Table of Contents

W9-AYY-637

Rocky Mountain News

Publisher, President & CEO: Larry Strutton
Editor: Robert W. Burdick
Managing Editor: John Temple
Book Editor: Chris Cubbison
Photo Editor: Janet Reeves **Sports Editor:** Barry Forbis
Writer: Bob Kravitz **Cartoonist:** Drew Litton
Photographers: Rodolfo Gonzalez, Cyrus McCrimmon, Hal Stoelzle,
Steve Dykes, Dennis Schroeder, Ken Papaleo, Ellen Jaskol,
Linda McConnell, Steven R. Nickerson, Glenn Asakawa,
Essdras M Suarez
Design and Production: Publication Design Inc.
Book Publisher: Johnson Books
Cover Photo: Avalanche star Joe Sakic, most valuable player
of the NHL playoffs, hoists the Stanley Cup after
Colorado's triple-overtime victory over Florida.
Photo by Cyrus McCrimmon.

Bringing Home the Cup

AVALANCHE!
CAPTURING THE CUP

By Bob Kravitz
and photographers of the
Rocky Mountain News

JOHNSON BOOKS • BOULDER

A Classy Championship

A championship can be won with class, or without it.

For the Colorado Avalanche, metro Denver and the state of Colorado, the 1996 Stanley Cup exemplified a championship with plenty of class.

How nice to read, hear and see the reactions of the Avalanche players after their heart-testing, triple-overtime victory in the deciding game of the Finals.

There was Patrick Roy, the stellar goalie who shared his confidence and often witty thoughts. And Joe Sakic, the team captain, whose reserve slipped away long enough for him to grin about the Cup, as well as his personal honor, the Conn Smythe Trophy.

Who couldn't be charmed by Adam Deadmarsh, the boyish winger who climbed atop a locker for the victory celebration? Or intrigued by Claude Lemieux, the feisty winger whose on-ice performance produced controversy as well as goals? Or reassured by Marc Crawford, only slightly less controlled than he had been throughout the season? Or cheered by the ebullient general manger, Pierre Lacroix?

PREVIOUS PAGE: Joe Sakic celebrates Uwe Krupp's Stanley Cup-winning goal against Florida.
Photo By Hal Stoelzle

And then, of course, there was almost any parent's favorite, Mike Ricci — the gritty player with the great smile, shaggy hair and missing teeth. He thanked his mother, pointing out how parents pay the bills for budding hockey stars and get them to practices, whether at dawn or late at night.

This book tells how these men and their teammates brought Denver its first major professional championship.

We thank all of them.

Bob Burdick, Editor
Rocky Mountain News

Drew Litton

Electrifying a joyous crowd on 17th Street, Avalanche team captain Joe Sakic lifts the Stanley Cup, symbolizing the first major pro sports championship in Colorado history.
Photo by Cyrus McCrimmon

LEFT: Mindell Reed unleashes a shower of confetti after the victory parade.
Photo by Steven R. Nickerson

RIGHT: Coach Marc Crawford revels in the adulation during a parade attended by a crowd estimated at a quarter-million or more.
Photo by Ken Papaleo

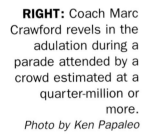

1995-1996 COLORADO AVALANCHE

May 24, 1995 — Quebec Nordiques owner Marcel Aubut sells the team for $75 million to Comsat, owner of the Denver Nuggets.

June 23 — Comsat solicits fans' help in picking the team's new name. The eight candidates: Avalanche, Rapids, Black Bears, Renegades, Cougars, Storm, Outlaws and Wranglers.

Aug. 10 — Comsat announces that the team will be called the Colorado Avalanche. The team colors will be burgundy, silver, blue and black.

Sept. 17 — In Cornwall, Ontario, the Avalanche plays its first exhibition game, losing 6-3 to the Montreal Canadiens.

Sept. 25 — In their home exhibition opener, the Avs beat the St. Louis Blues 3-1. It marks the NHL's return to the ice in Denver after an absence of 14 years.

Oct. 3 — The Avalanche acquires tough-guy winger Claude Lemieux from the New Jersey Devils.

Oct. 6 — The Avs win their regular-season opener, beating the Detroit Red Wings 3-2 at soldout McNichols Arena.

Oct. 26 — Avs acquire defenseman Sandis Ozol from the Sa Jose Sharks bolster the team's scor punch.

ABOVE: Fans pack Civic Center to cheer Avalanche players and coaches on the steps of the City and County Building.

Photo by Ellen Jaskol

FIRST-YEAR MILESTONES

Dec. 6 — The Avs land superstar goalie Patrick Roy and forward Mike Keane in a blockbuster trade with the Montreal Canadiens. "This is the man who can take us to the Stanley Cup," Avs general manager Pierre Lacroix says about Roy.

Feb. 19, 1996 — Roy becomes the 12th goalie in NHL history to record 300 career victories as the Avalanche beats Edmonton 7-5.

April 14 — Avalanche ends the regular season with a 5-4 loss to the Los Angeles Kings, finishing at 47-25-10.

April 27 — Avalanche beats Vancouver 3-2 to win its first round of the playoffs, 4 games to 2.

May 13 — Avalanche beats Chicago 4-3 to win Round Two, 4 games to 2.

May 29 — Avalanche beats Detroit 4-1 to win Western Conference finals, 4 games to 2.

June 10 — Avalanche beats Florida 1-0 in triple overtime to sweep the Stanley Cup Finals, 4 games to 0.

June 12 — A quarter-million fans jam downtown Denver to salute the Avalanche, the first major professional sports champion in Colorado history.

4:31 into 3rd OT = 1 Stanley Cup

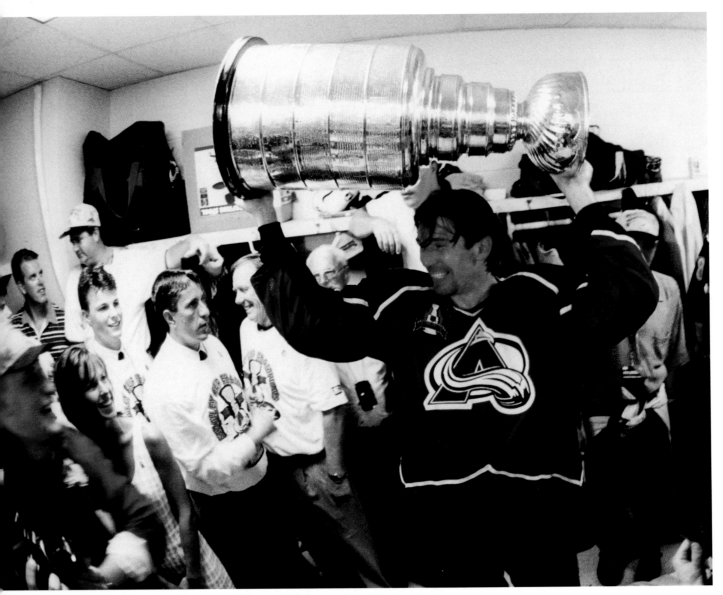

ABOVE: Uwe Krupp, who scored the goal that won the Stanley Cup, holds the revered trophy in the locker room after his moment of destiny.
Photo by Rodolfo Gonzalez

ABOVE: Claude Lemieux (above, center) erupts with joy after scoring the first goal in Game 3 of the Finals, powering the Avalanche toward a sweep.
Photo by Hal Stoelzle

RIGHT: As Game 4 turns pressure-cooker on the ice in Miami, tension grips Avs fans in Denver. Stephanie Smith holds her head and Wendy Donohue crosses her fingers at the Sports Column bar in LoDo.
Photo by Dennis Schroeder

They call him St. Patrick, and Patrick Roy shows why, diving to block a shot in Game 4 by Florida's Mike Hough. Roy stopped an astounding 63 shots in the Avs' triple-overtime 1-0 victory that clinched the Cup.

Photo by Hal Stoelzle

ABOVE: Avs addicts celebrate victory outside the Sports Column bar in LoDo.
Photo by Dennis Schroeder

ABOVE: Plastic rats tossed onto the ice in Miami by Panthers fans mark one of Florida's few good moments.
Photo by Hal Stoelzle

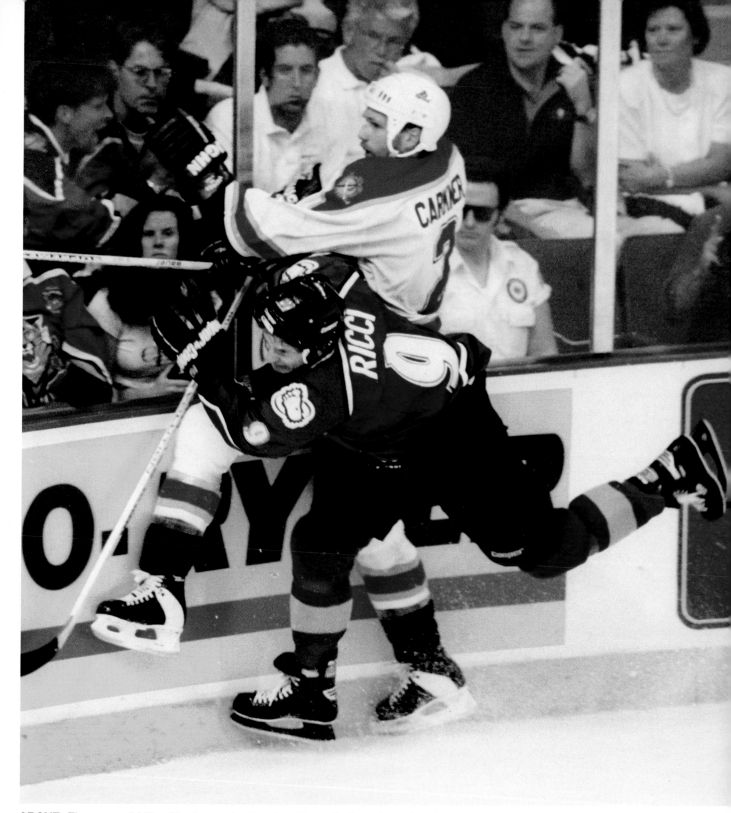

ABOVE: The rugged Mike Ricci smacks Panther Terry Carkner into the glass at Miami Arena. Plays like this squelched any doubts that Avalanche players were tough enough to win the Stanley Cup.
Photo by Rodolfo Gonzalez

ABOVE: Swarming the Stanley Cup, the Avs celebrate their crowning achievement.
Photo by Hal Stoelzle

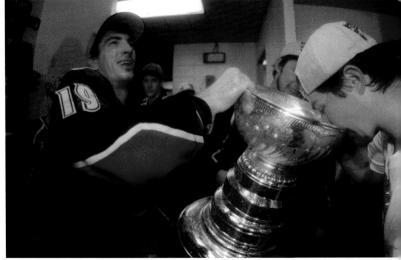

RIGHT: Stephane Yelle sips champagne from the Cup as Joe Sakic lends a steadying hand.
Photo by Rodolfo Gonzalez

ABOVE: Avalanche captain Joe Sakic skates away with the Conn Smythe Trophy after being honored as the most valuable player of the playoffs.

Photo by Hal Stoelzle

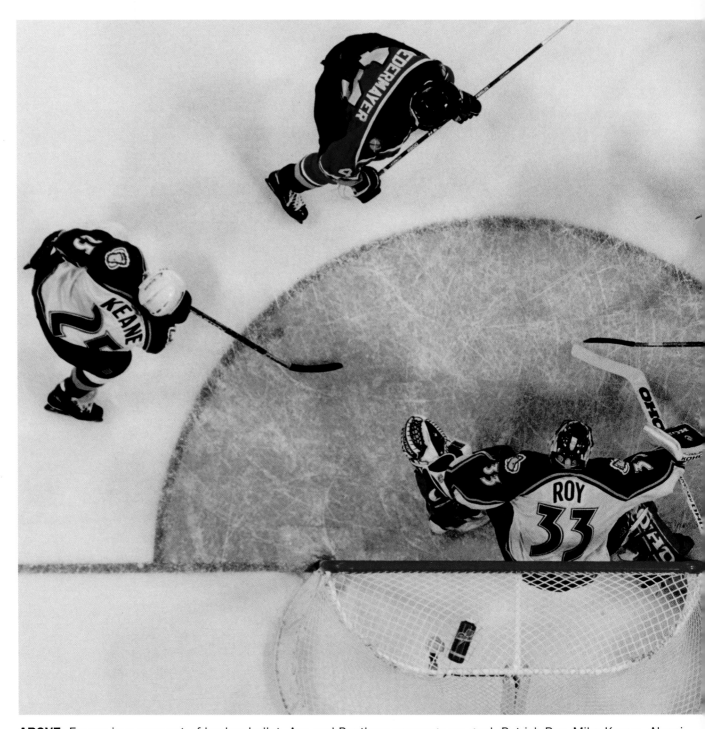

ABOVE: Frozen in a moment of hockey ballet, Avs and Panthers converge on goal. Patrick Roy, Mike Keane, Alexei Gusarov and Adam Foote guard the Avs' net while Scott Mellanby and Rob Niedermayer fight for an opening.
Photo by Hal Stoelzle

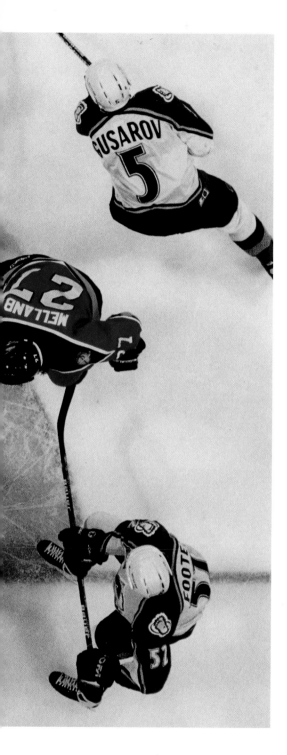

RIGHT: Denver fans created their own avalanche of puns based on the French pronunciation of goalie Patrick Roy's name (WAH).
Photo by Ken Papaleo

17

Celebration!

Avalanche fan(atic) Ted (he won't tell us his last name) is lifted toward the heavens by Mike Grigsby after Mike Ricci's goal in Colorado's 4-1 victory over the Detroit Red Wings May 29. The win gave the Avs the Western Conference title and put them in the Stanley Cup Finals against the Florida Panthers.
Photo by Rodolfo Gonzalez

Avalanche fever sweeps Colorado

"How good does it feel, Colorado?"
— **Mike Haynes**, radio play-by-play man, after Uwe Krupp's goal won the Stanley Cup for the Colorado Avalanche.

Thirty-six years.

From dusty old cowtown to boom to bust to boom again, Denver had never known the unbridled joy that comes with a major professional sports championship.

The Broncos had come so close so many times, only to lose four Super Bowls. The Nuggets once sniffed a title during their American Basketball Association days, then reached the Western Conference finals twice after joining the NBA. And the Rockies, born in 1993, captivated Colorado by making the baseball playoffs as a wild-card team in 1995.

Then came the Avalanche.

The . . . who?

The Avalanche.

In just one season in Denver, the heroes of hockey gave Colorado's long-suffering fans their Holy Grail.

How good does it feel?

Eons of failure suddenly melted from memory. The result: a primal scream unlike any the town and state had ever heard.

Two days after the Avalanche completed its sweep of the Florida Panthers with a triple-overtime, 1-0 victory in Miami, Denver held the party it had longed to throw ever since the Broncos were born in 1960.

The Avalanche paraded the Stanley Cup, the most treasured trophy in sports, through downtown Denver, finishing with a wild celebration on the

RIGHT: Panthers crowds had their plastic rats, but Avs fanatics had their rat traps, especially at McNichols Sports Arena during Game 2.
Photo by Rodolfo Gonzalez

"Stand still! Smile! Say cheese!" Fans young and old posed with the Stanley Cup as the Finals came to Denver. Mark Lu, 5, straightens up for his picture at the Westminster Mall J.C. Penney store.
Photo by Essdras M Suarez

steps of the City and County Building.

The raucous crowd, estimated at a quarter-million or more, stretched as far as the eye could see.

The mood was electric.

"I didn't know Denver had this many people," Avalanche defenseman Adam Foote marveled, standing atop a firetruck, holding a cigar and a beer.

Then, captain Joe Sakic, the team's finest player, grabbed the microphone and said, "Denver has the greatest fans in sports."

And who could argue?

The love between team and fans had been one whirlwind romance.

It started tentatively in October when the transplanted team began its inaugural season in Denver.

The ardor picked up steam in November when the Avalanche first served notice it was going to be one of the league's elite teams. By the time the Avs were entangled with the Chicago Blackhawks in the second round of the Stanley Cup playoffs, Denver was just plain head over heels.

The Avs did more than enthrall with their tough, steady play and phenomenal Stanley Cup run; they enraptured Denver with their grace, humility and passion.

Folks who wouldn't have known Mike Ricci from pasta fagioli six months earlier held up signs proposing marriage. People who might have thought Marc Crawford a button-down corporate lawyer now demanded a long-term contract for the coach.

As the ticker-tape parade made its way down Broadway, general manager Pierre Lacroix leaned over a railing on his firetruck and led a sidewalk chorus of "Stanley Cup! Stanley Cup!"

Then came Crawford, hair in place as always,

ABOVE: Strange growths sprout atop the heads of Avalanche fans as Cup fever descends on Denver. Imitation Stanley Cups are all the rage — until the Avs bring home the real thing.
Photo by Cyrus McCrimmon

standing tall, waving to the adoring multitudes. Then came the players, those who had been post-season stars — Sakic, Patrick Roy and Peter Forsberg — and those who hadn't — Craig Wolanin, Chris Simon, Stephane Fiset.

The crowning moments were shared by family — the wives, the kids, the parents.

The players talked not about endorsement deals or paychecks but about the Cup and the family support that helped them reach the summit. Who would have imagined it?

Everybody around the National Hockey League thought the Nordiques-turned-Avs were good, filled with prime, young talent.

But were they ready?

Were they rugged and experienced enough to capture a Stanley Cup? In their final season as the Quebec Nordiques, these players had turned the corner, going 30-13-5, only to fall to the New York Rangers in the first round of the playoffs. But by the time the Avalanche showed up for the 1996 playoffs, it was a tougher team, infused by what Lacroix liked to call "winning blood," the result of three seismic trades.

Then began the blitzkrieg toward the Cup. For the fans, it was a two-month joyride, for the players, a marathon of ballet and bonecrushing.

By the time Uwe Krupp's seemingly harmless slapshot from the point slipped past Florida's John Vanbiesbrouck 4:31 into the third overtime — third overtime! — the epic journey was done.

Four games and out, and Colorado had its first major pro sports champion.

How good did it feel?

Good.

Real good.

LEFT: The confetti ladies of 17th Street deluge the Parade of Champions.
Photo by Cyrus McCrimmon

Ready to stop just about anything, a young fan enters McNichols Arena to cheer on goaltender Patrick Roy.
Photo by Steven R. Nickerson

24

Fireworks bathe the City and County Building in fiery splendor as Avs star Joe Sakic presents the Stanley Cup to an exuberant crowd of well-wishers.
Photo by Linda McConnell

In perhaps the most controversial moment of the playoffs, Avs winger Claude Lemieux crushes Detroit's Kris Draper from behind in Game 6 of the Western Conference finals. The hit, which cost Lemieux a two-game suspension, left Draper with a broken nose and jaw.
Photo by Rodolfo Gonzalez

LEFT: Avs fans signal their support of Lemieux.
Photo by Cyrus McCrimmon

BELOW: The Avalanche's Scott Young sends Florida's Rhett Warrener flying during Game 3 in Miami.
Photo by Hal Stoelzle

27

ABOVE: When he's not blanketing the net, Patrick Roy finds other ways to frustrate opponents, as in this move on Detroit's Dino Ciccarelli.

LEFT: The legendary goaltender even makes a water break look like a work of art.
Photos by Steve Dykes

ABOVE: A study in intensity, Peter Forsberg prepares to pounce.
Photo by Cyrus McCrimmon

RIGHT: Mike Ricci takes no prisoners with his aggressive game. Before the season, hockey experts wondered if the Avs were rough and tough enough to win the Cup. Bringing the hammer down in the Finals, the Avs killed off any doubt.
Photo by Hal Stoelzle

The Stanley Cup. The Avalanche. The state capitol. The Denver skyline.
And tens of thousands of proud fans. They all come together in the glorious
Colorado twilight, a sports moment for the ages.
Photo by Ken Papaleo

Bienvenue, Nordiques

They could have been the Outlaws or the Renegades, but the
Quebec Nordiques became the Colorado Avalanche. Fans
helped choose the name. Shawn Hunter, then the marketing
chief for the newly transplanted team, explains the rules.

Avalanche
Black Bears
Cougars
Outlaws
Rapids
Renegades
Storm
Wranglers

WHAT'S IN A NAME?

SEND YOUR COMMENTS BY FAX TO 893-0014 OR MA

Denver lands the Nordiques

The story of the Avalanche's march to the Stanley Cup was remarkable enough, but no more remarkable — or unlikely — than the team's move to Denver.

How did it get here?

Well, it was not the result of some concerted civic effort. The Denver sports calendar was already pretty well-rounded, especially with the Broncos, the Nuggets and the 1993 arrival of baseball's expansion Rockies.

For the time being, folks seemed happy enough with the minor-league Denver Grizzlies, who would draw nice crowds and win the International Hockey League's Turner Cup in 1994-95, their first and only year in town.

And be honest: While Denver had a long and varied hockey history, it wasn't exactly brimming with success stories. Beginning in 1950, the Denver Falcons, Denver Mavericks, Denver Invaders and Denver Spurs filled the years, in fits and

starts, with minor-league hockey. But the teams were gone almost as soon as they had arrived.

The National Hockey League finally made it to Denver with the sad and befuddling, if occasionally exciting, Colorado Rockies. They came to town in 1976 as the Kansas City Scouts and left six years later to become the New Jersey Devils. In the interim, they were sabotaged by mismanagement, multiple ownership and a lack of funds, especially from what they bemoaned was a bad lease at McNichols Sports Arena.

A decade later, efforts to bring the NHL back began. In the background — the deep background — Comsat, the owner of the Denver Nuggets, started expanding the company's sports and entertainment base. That meant strengthening basketball and luring an NHL team to play in a planned, privately financed arena.

The plans of Comsat and Ascent, its new sports and entertainment arm, coincided beautifully with

ABOVE: Avalanche players listen to coach Marc Crawford at a meet-the-media briefing shortly after the team moved to Denver.
Photo by Cyrus McCrimmon

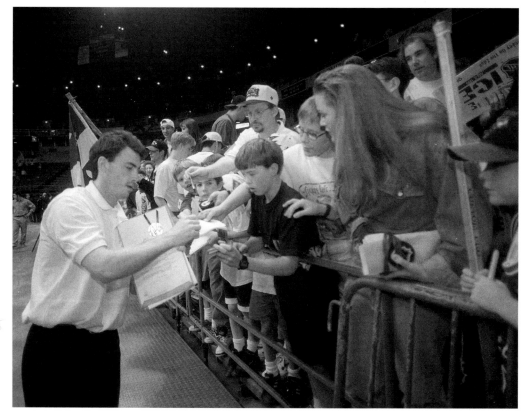

LEFT: Joe Sakic signs autographs in McNichols Arena as fans welcome the team to Colorado.
Photo by Cyrus McCrimmon

ABOVE: The return of big-league hockey to Denver sent legions of kids into the streets with newly minted sticks, jerseys, roller blades and helmets.
Photo by Cyrus McCrimmon

the NHL's long-term vision.

Convenient, eh?

It was 1993 and former National Basketball Association executive Gary Bettman had just taken over as NHL commissioner. Bettman knew about Comsat and Ascent. He also knew Ascent's president, Charlie Lyons, from their NBA days and thought Denver might be a suitable spot for a future hockey franchise.

It didn't matter to Bettman that the old hockey Rockies had a short and often unhappy tenure in Denver. What he knew was this: Denver had grown both as a city and sports market, Denver had great demographics, Denver had produced

some of the best TV ratings among non-NHL cities and, more than anything, Denver had Comsat.

"He called us from the moment he began with the NHL," Lyons said. "He said, 'Look, you guys have done a great job cleaning up a real mess with the Nuggets. Denver would be a great city for the league, and you're the right group if the NHL were to come to Denver.'"

At that point, Lyons figured he was embarking on a mission to bring an expansion team to Denver around 1998, coinciding with what he hoped would be the opening of the new Pepsi Center. His company, he thought, would be a stalking horse, helping the NHL solve some of its weak franchise

On opening night of the 1995-96 regular season, Peter Alston, 11, of Littleton, has his picture taken behind a huge cutout of an Avalanche player.
Photo by Glenn Asakawa

37

problems by giving club owners leverage in their attempts to get new buildings.

Recalled Lyons:

"They told us, 'If you're willing to put your reputation on the line and are willing to be left at the altar a few times, it's probably worthwhile because ultimately, you'll get married to the NHL.' "

Who knew such a happy marriage was in the works?

Nobody.

In fact, the chase for an NHL franchise actually started in Hartford, where the Whalers were desperate for an owner who would keep them in Connecticut. Comsat wasn't terribly interested but was willing to help the NHL as a potential bailout.

Luckily — and fortunately for Denver — the Whalers were saved by another owner.

Then Bettman called again, this time in the winter of 1994, and set up a meeting between Lyons and Quebec Nordiques owner Marcel Aubut.

Aubut was having difficulty convincing city and provincial leaders to help him build a new arena to replace the aging Le Colisee. Worse, the Nordiques were playing in the league's smallest market. Aubut insisted he could not compete in the modern-day NHL playing in that building.

If Quebec could not take care of him, might

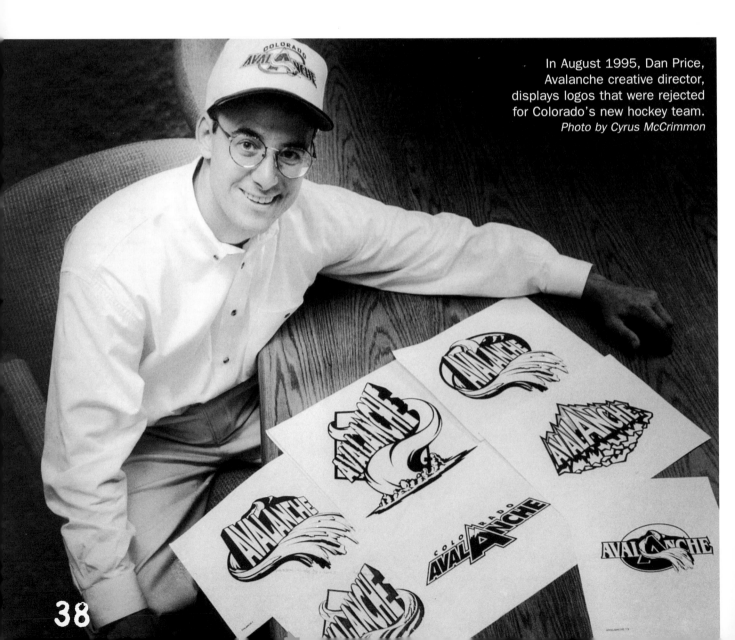

In August 1995, Dan Price, Avalanche creative director, displays logos that were rejected for Colorado's new hockey team.
Photo by Cyrus McCrimmon

38

Comsat be interested in buying, and moving, his franchise?

"I thought, 'There ain't no chance,' " Lyons said. "It was very clear from the beginning Marcel wanted nothing more than to keep his team in Quebec."

But Lyons met with Aubut anyway, fully expecting Quebec officials to capitulate to Aubut's demands.

Then came a phone call in April 1995, shortly after the Nordiques' playoff loss to the Rangers.

"It's over," Aubut told Lyons. "The (Quebec) government has not responded."

And the Denver deal was done, $75 million to purchase this fine young team and its minor-league affiliate in Cornwall, Ontario. The process deeply pained Aubut; he would make a financial killing, but this team was his life's passion.

Now, it would be part of Colorado's sporting life, the final piece making Denver one of nine cities boasting four major professional teams.

As Aubut completed the transaction, he told Lyons, "Denver has no idea what it's about to get."

How prophetic he was.

ABOVE: Avalanche player Mike Ricci gets a high-five greeting from Rocky, the Denver Nuggets mascot, at a McNichols Arena welcome rally on July 5, 1995.
Photo by Cyrus McCrimmon

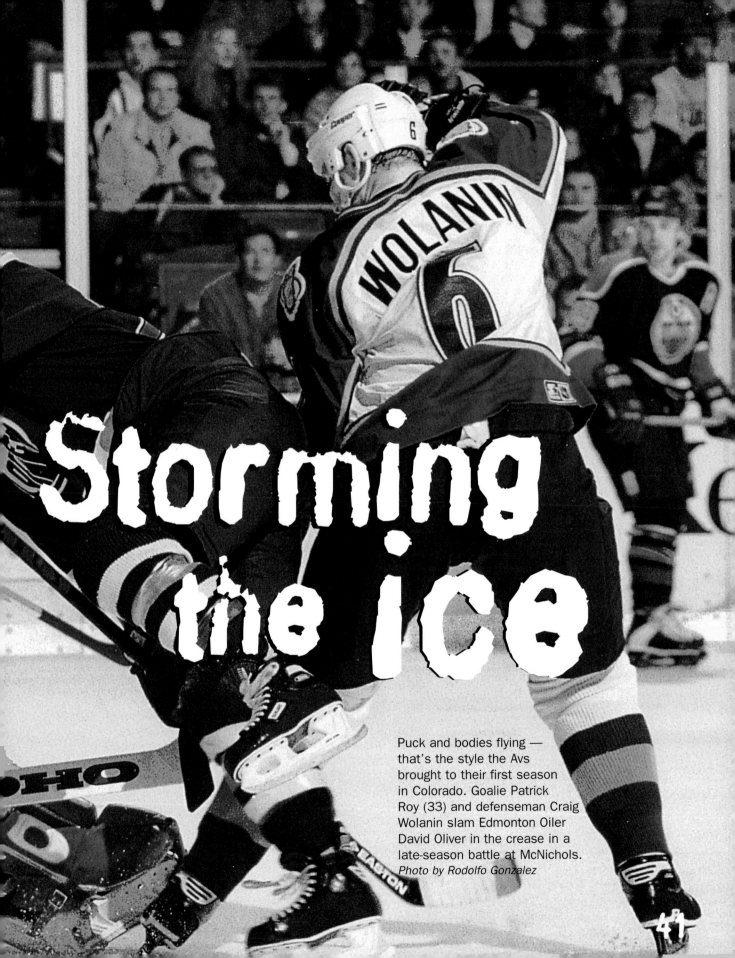

Storming the ice

Puck and bodies flying — that's the style the Avs brought to their first season in Colorado. Goalie Patrick Roy (33) and defenseman Craig Wolanin slam Edmonton Oiler David Oliver in the crease in a late-season battle at McNichols. *Photo by Rodolfo Gonzalez*

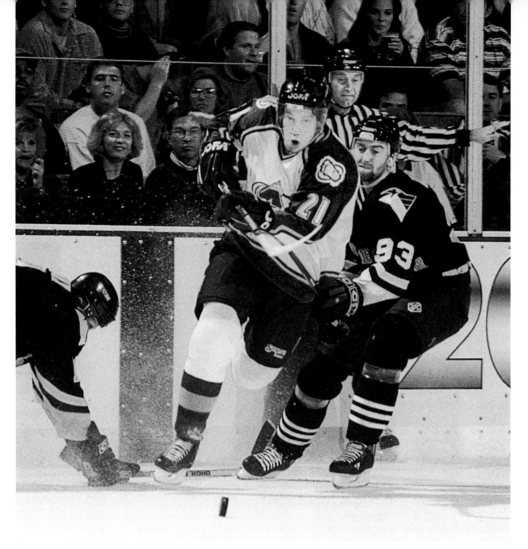

RIGHT: Center Peter Forsberg hurtles toward the puck, leaving Pittsburgh Penguins center Petr Nedved behind.
Photo by Dennis Schroeder

The First Season

One persistent question accompanied the National Hockey League's triumphant return to Denver:

"Who are these Avalanche guys, anyway?"

When the team was introduced Oct. 6 for its first home game against the Detroit Red Wings at jam-packed McNichols Arena, few knew what these players and coaches were all about.

Sylvain Lefebvre? Adam Foote? Marc Crawford? This was a mystery team, having toiled in relative obscurity in Quebec City.

Hockey purists told us it was a team on the edge of something special, a collection of young, untamed talent that had been built by the Eric Lindros trade and a succession of top-5 draft choices.

The old Nordiques had been so bad for so long. Now, rebuilding, they had forged the second-best record in hockey in the lockout-shortened 1994-95 season — only to lose to the New York Rangers in six games in the first round of the playoffs.

When the Nordiques were purchased by Comsat and moved to Denver, Quebec City hockey writer Kevin Johnston told the Rocky Mountain News, "You have a team that is very close to winning a Stanley Cup."

Nobody knew how close.

The inaugural regular season in Denver was a success by any measure — a 47-25-10 record, second-best in the game behind the Red Wings. There were some memorable moments — notably the nationally televised 7-1 massacre of the

LEFT: Fists flying, Avalanche winger Warren Rychel battles Scott Daniels of the Hartford Whalers during a game Feb. 9.
Photo by Ellen Jaskol

BELOW: Goaltender Patrick Roy hooks Todd Marchant of the Edmonton Oilers during an 8-1 Avalanche victory March 17.
Photo by Rodolfo Gonzalez

43

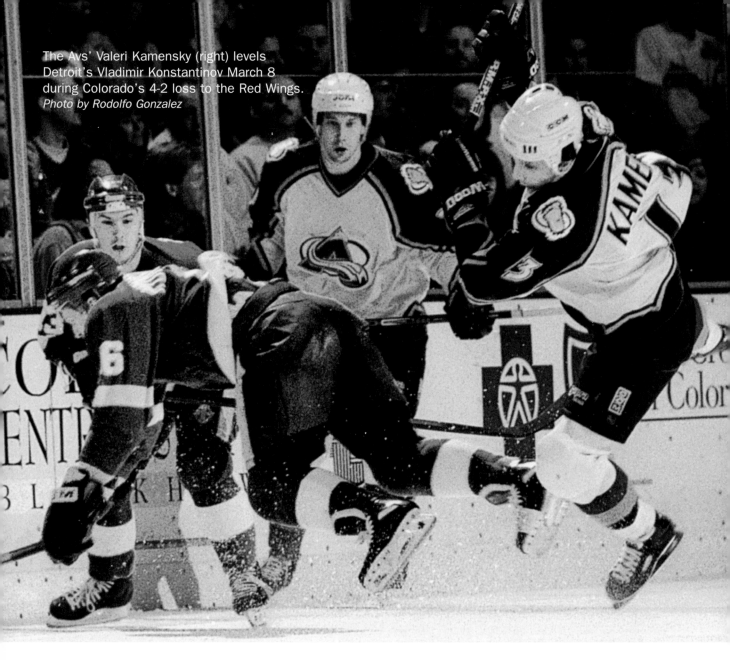

The Avs' Valeri Kamensky (right) levels Detroit's Vladimir Konstantinov March 8 during Colorado's 4-2 loss to the Red Wings.
Photo by Rodolfo Gonzalez

Rangers Feb. 3.

But a certain urgency was missing. The team had no competition in the weakened Pacific Division, and by mid-season it was clear the Avalanche would finish behind torrid Detroit and ahead of third-place Chicago in the Western Conference.

The important thing, Coach Marc Crawford kept saying, was that his team keep "piling on good habits" and get itself prepared for the real season — the playoffs, the road to the Stanley Cup.

While the Avalanche players came to know their new city and the city came to know the players, the biggest news came off the ice.

General manager Pierre Lacroix believed the Avalanche was missing three key ingredients to compete seriously for the Stanley Cup:

■ A time-tested, playoff-savvy goaltender.

■ An offensive defenseman who could quarterback the power play and offer scoring punch from the backline.

■ Physical, nasty, gritty character players who would sell their soul for a Stanley Cup.

So Lacroix, who had left a successful sports consulting company to become general manager one year earlier, went to work.

And in the process, he turned the hockey world, and the Avalanche, upside down.

ABOVE: Avs enforcer Chris Simon has his
fists ready for Doug Zmolek of the Los Angeles Kings
during Colorado's 6-2 victory Feb. 23.
Photo by Rodolfo Gonzalez

RIGHT: A key early-season trade brought
the scoring punch of defenseman
Sandis Ozolinsh to the Avs.
Photo by Dennis Schroeder

On Oct. 3, just three days before the start of
the regular season, Lacroix had had enough of
Wendel Clark's contract holdout. He traded the
veteran winger and team leader to the New Jersey Devils in a three-team trade that brought the
notorious Claude Lemieux to the Avalanche.

Lemieux was one of the toughest, nastiest,
most abrasive players in the league, a two-time
Cup winner who had earned the Conn Smythe
Trophy a year earlier with the New Jersey Devils
as the most valuable player in the playoffs.

Less than a month later, the need for an
offensive defenseman made even more pressing
by Uwe Krupp's opening-night knee injury,

45

Lacroix dealt one of the league's best wingers, Owen Nolan, to the San Jose Sharks for Sandis Ozolinsh, a young Latvian defenseman with mountains of skill.

Like the Lemieux deal, this trade raised eyebrows. Nolan was a long-time Nordique, a centerpiece of a team that had gone from futility to contention. And Ozolinsh hadn't always lived up to expectations.

The trade of Nolan, one of the team's primary scorers and leaders, sent shock waves through a club that thought it already was on the fast track to greatness.

"There's no doubt in my mind those major trades woke the guys up," Crawford said. "For one, when we went out and got Claude, I think the guys said, 'Whoa, these people are serious about winning.'

"And the same thing with Owen, who grew up in this organization. That was a very hard trade to make — very hard. But we knew what we were missing. And again, I think the players saw that and said, 'Our management is going to do what it takes.' "

But the real blockbuster deal was yet to be made.

On Dec. 2, legendary Montreal goaltender Patrick Roy was getting shelled by the Red

ABOVE: Patrick Roy and the rest of the Avs took Denver sports fans by storm, horning in on the adulation once reserved solely for Broncos quarterback John Elway.
Photo by Rodolfo Gonzalez

Wings, giving up nine goals in less than two periods. The longer the bombardment continued, the angrier Roy got.

Why, he wondered, wasn't new coach Mario Tremblay pulling him out to save him from this embarrassment? Hadn't he done enough for Montreal, winning two Conn Smythe trophies and two Stanley Cups, to be given that courtesy?

When Roy finally left the net, he blew past Tremblay and told team president Ronald Corey, "That's my last game for the organization."

The Montreal braintrust decided, then and there, to end the long and mostly happy marriage between Roy and the Canadiens.

It took Lacroix all of three seconds to get interested. Not only did he want an experienced goalie, but Roy had once been his client. He was like a son.

On Dec. 6, the trade was made: Roy and forward Mike Keane for left wing Martin Rucinsky, right wing Andrei Kovalenko and promising young goalie Jocelyn Thibault.

"This is the man who can take us to the Stanley Cup," Lacroix said of Roy.

Three months.

Three deals.

The face of the Avalanche had been changed forever.

But the best memories were yet to come.

Patrick Roy deflects a shot off his leg Feb. 3 during the Avs' nationally televised 7-1 rout of the New York Rangers.
Photo by Rodolfo Gonzalez

47

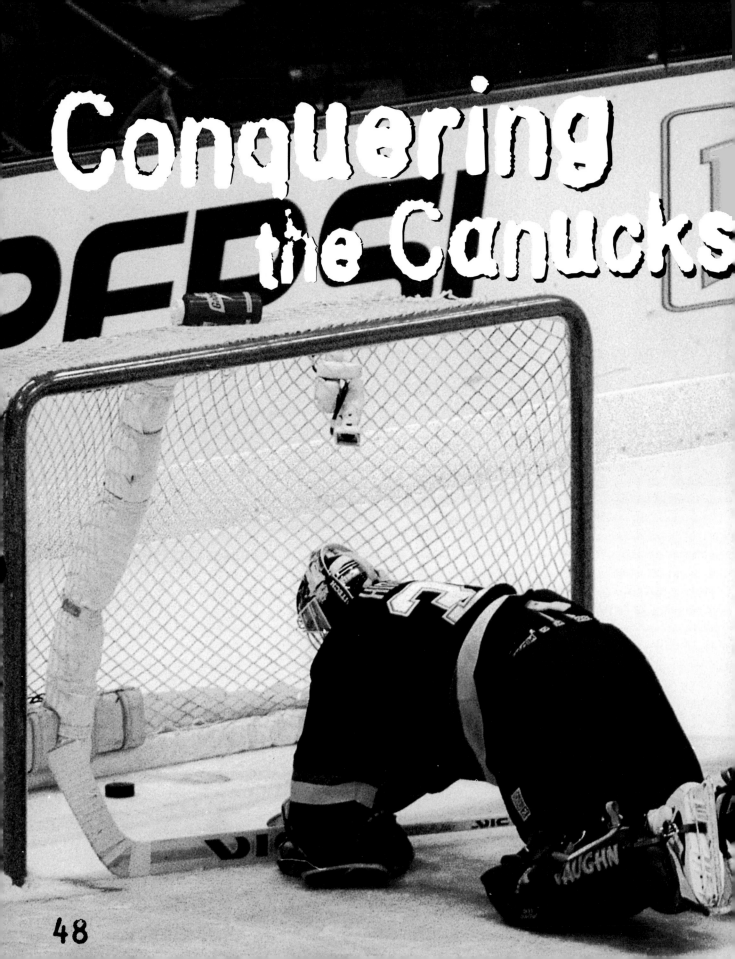

Conquering the Canucks

Avs winger Valeri Kamensky celebrates his goal in Game 1. Canucks goaltender Corey Hirsch stares helplessly at the puck that got by him.
Photo by Cyrus McCrimmon

Playoffs, Round One: Vancouver

The playoffs.

In hockey, more than any other professional sport, the playoffs are, indeed, a new season.

The intensity increases tenfold. The style of play changes dramatically. A wide-open, offensive game gives way to a more physical, close-checking style. That is why, in the playoffs, defense and goaltending win.

The Avalanche was well positioned to make a run at the Cup when it learned, on the final day of the regular season, that it would play the dangerous Vancouver Canucks in the first round.

"I like where we are," Coach Marc Crawford said on the eve of the playoffs. "We've shown we can play the kind of hockey you need in the playoffs."

But could the Avalanche, the second-highest scoring team in the league yet just its ninth-best defensively, play the close-to-the-vest game it took to win in the playoffs?

Could superstar goalie Patrick Roy, who had been just ordinary in the regular season, raise his game yet again and lead the Avalanche to the Stanley Cup?

More than anything, was this team ready to purge the ghosts of playoff failures past? Or would it be haunted by last season's surprising six-game loss to the New York Rangers in the first round?

While the Vancouver Canucks had sneaked into seventh place in the conference on the final day of the season, they were a veteran, dangerous team that had taken a .500 record into the playoffs two years earlier and streaked into the Stanley Cup Finals.

Sure, center Pavel Bure would not play because of an injury, but the Canucks still had the great scorer, Alexander Mogilny, and Kirk McLean, the goaltender who led the Canucks to the Cup Finals in 1994.

In Game 1, the Avalanche played as advertised. The stars stepped up the way Crawford had hoped — Peter Forsberg, Valeri Kamensky, Claude Lemieux and, especially, Roy.

Forsberg's game-tying goal late in the first

LEFT: Mike Ricci closes in on the puck against the Canucks.
Photo by Hal Stoelzle

RIGHT: Defenseman Uwe Krupp fought back from a disastrous knee injury in the season opener and rejoined the team for the playoff run.
Photo by Hal Stoelzle

period set up a devastating second-period assault — goals by Kamensky, Joe Sakic and Sandis Ozolinsh. More important, the onslaught helped chase McLean, who looked unusually shaky.

When it was over, the Avalanche had set the stage for what figured to be a long, wild post-season ride with a 5-2 victory.

But two nights later, the soft, sloppy Avalanche team that had sometimes emerged during the regular season showed up. As Game 2 unfolded, it was fair to wonder if the Avalanche was, indeed, ready to take that next step.

The Avs were undone by Gino Odjick, the gap-toothed Vancouver enforcer who had no points and 100 penalty minutes in 26 previous playoff games. Odjick not only flattened Colorado's Troy Murray with a cross-check that went unpenalized, he scored two crippling goals.

The Avalanche lost 5-4, leaving the series even at one game apiece. But a turning point in the Avs' drive to the Stanley Cup was about to occur.

The morning after Game 2, the Avalanche heard about comments Vancouver head coach and general manager Pat Quinn made after Game 1. He had bemoaned his team's failure to storm the Colorado net, to attack Avalanche defensemen he branded "a bunch of marshmallows."

Crawford then gave his team a tongue-lashing during practice, questioning their toughness and commitment.

It didn't stop there. Avalanche winger/enforcer Chris Simon apparently made a gesture during Crawford's tirade, triggering an even angrier diatribe at Simon, who hadn't done anything the night before to avenge Odjick's nasty

ABOVE: Chris Simon (12) and the rest of the Avs endured a harsh scolding from Coach Marc Crawford after Game 2 against Vancouver. Crawford's tirade spurred the team.
Photo by Hal Stoelzle

hit on Murray. By the end of practice, a disgraced Simon could be found on hands and knees, alone behind a net.

Angry and chastened, Colorado played nearly a perfect game, beating Vancouver 4-0 in GM Place. The power play produced three goals, the penalty-killing units neutralized a pair of two-man disadvantages and Roy was solid as a fortress.

Marshmallows? Hardly.

"I thought Crow (Crawford) made a great decision doing that," defenseman Adam Foote said of the head coach's heated state-of-the-union address. "I thought what he did brought us together. He put us in a position where we either stuck together or crumbled."

But the motivation seemed to last just 24 hours. The Canucks tied the series 2-2 with a 4-3 victory in Vancouver. The power play was non-existent, Odjick was back in the Avs' faces and the defense gave up turnovers.

Was it time for another Crawford explosion?

No, it was time for Sakic to begin staking his

claim to the Conn Smythe Trophy. Game 5 in Denver was Sakic's moment, and it established him as more than a great talent. Sakic clearly was now a player who could single-handedly win hockey games.

Trailing 4-2 deep in the third period, the season on the line, the Avalanche got a goal from rarely used left wing Rene Corbet, then saw Sakic tie the score with 5:53 left. It was his second goal of the game.

Next, just 51 seconds into overtime, Sakic let loose with his patented wrist shot from an impossible angle beyond the faceoff circle and near the boards. The puck sailed between Corey Hirsch's pads and into the net.

The Avalanche's great escape was complete. Later, Colorado defenseman Uwe Krupp would say, "That was the turning point of the playoffs."

The Avalanche quickly put the finishing touches on the Canucks, winning Game 6 in Vancouver 3-2 on (guess who?) Sakic's late goal.

"Don't look for them ghosts," Roy said in a jubilant locker room. "Those ghosts, they ain't here."

Blackhawks

Hand-to-hand combat like this breakaway between Avs captain Joe Sakic and
Blackhawks goalie Eddie Belfour made the Colorado-Chicago series unforgettable.
Photo by Steve Dykes

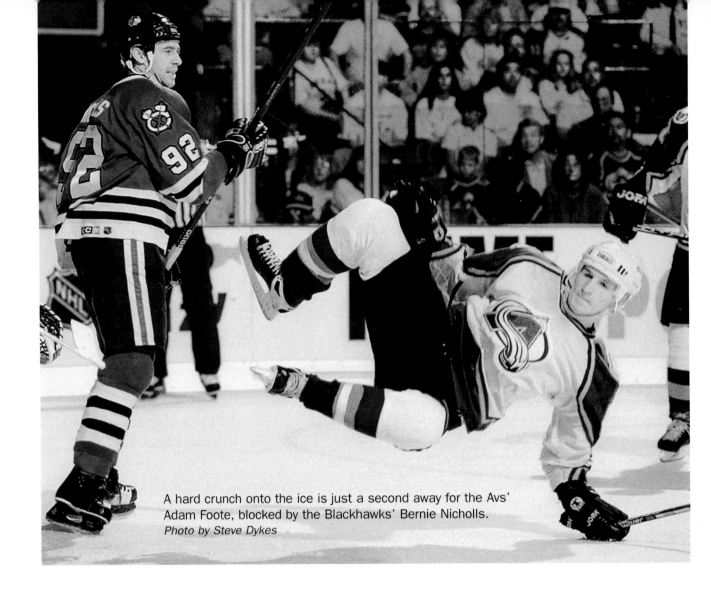

A hard crunch onto the ice is just a second away for the Avs' Adam Foote, blocked by the Blackhawks' Bernie Nicholls.
Photo by Steve Dykes

Playoffs, Round Two: Chicago

This chapter will be a little longer than most.

In fact, you could say it's going into overtime.

That would only be appropriate in recounting the long, brutish struggle between the Avalanche and the storied Chicago Blackhawks in the second round of the Stanley Cup playoffs.

Working overtime? Check this out: Four of the six games went overtime. Two needed one overtime. A third game went double OT. And then there was epic, triumphant triple-overtime Game 4 in Chicago, a decisive moment in the Avalanche's

march to the Cup.

Along the way, hockey fans got as good a show off the ice as on.

There were officiating controversies. There was the loss of Chicago goalie Eddie Belfour and winger Murray Craven in Game 2 because, they said, they suffered food poisoning after eating at a Denver restaurant. There was Enrico Ciccone, getting into it with fans and a Denver policeman. There was Chicago winger Tony Amonte's devastating injury. There was The Equipment Affair:

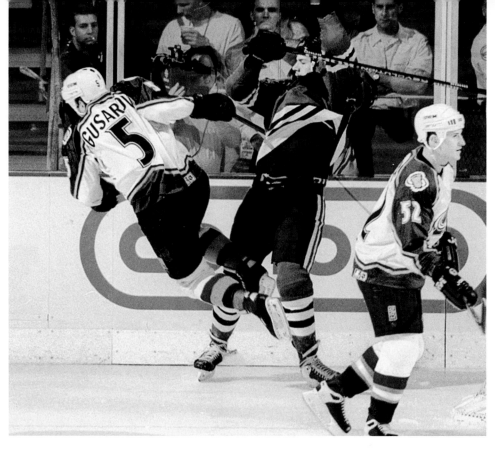

LEFT: Avalanche defenseman Alexei Gusarov collides with Blackhawk Steve Smith in Game 5.
Photo by Hal Stoelzle

BELOW: Joe Sakic's popularity with Avalanche fans went off the charts during the playoffs, as these charter members of the Sakic Fan Club will attest.
Photo by Cyrus McCrimmon

57

ABOVE: Center Dave Hannan celebrates an Avalanche goal in Game 5. Four of the six games in the dramatic Colorado-Chicago series went into overtime.
Photo by Steve Dykes

When Chris Chelios sat out Game 4, the Blackhawks said he had "an equipment problem." He really had a pulled groin muscle.

And there were overtimes . . . all those overtimes.

The series began quietly — and ominously for the Avalanche — with the Hawks winning 3-2 on Jeremy Roenick's overtime goal. Suddenly, the Avalanche was back in trouble, especially against a big, aggressive team with a great goaltender and one of the league's best records.

But the Avalanche rebounded, thanks in part

to what the Hawks called food poisoning. (The truth is a rare commodity during the playoffs.) Whatever the case, Belfour and Craven could not play, and the Avalanche dominated. Valeri Kamensky, Craig Wolanin, Joe Sakic and Uwe Krupp scored on replacement goalie Jeff Hackett within a span of 5:44 to take a commanding 4-1 first-period lead.

The Avs never looked back. The biggest excitement came later, when Chicago tough guy Ciccone was tossed from the game and responded to taunting by pawing at a fan, then scuffling with a Denver policeman.

That brought the series to Chicago, home of the world's loudest and most passionate fans. There is no sound in all of sports like the cosmic howl produced by the city's leather lungs during the national anthem. The only problem: the Blackhawks didn't come out with the same fire as their fans.

The Avalanche led 3-1 after two periods on goals by Sakic, Peter Forsberg and Mike Ricci. But the Avalanche, who never blew leads all year except against the Blackhawks, could not hold on. The Hawks stormed back, tied the score in regulation, then won early in overtime on Wolanin's giveaway and Sergei Krivokrasov's fluttering shot over Patrick Roy's shoulder.

The Avs were down two games to one and peering at serious trouble if they lost Game 4. Lose here, and it was 3-1 Chicago and the playoff run was likely done. Win here, and Colorado again had the home-ice advantage.

Chelios, the Blackhawks' great defenseman and captain, attempted to skate during warmups. When he wasn't on the bench for the start of Game 4, the Hawks announced he had "an equipment problem." The real reason: The team doctor had given Chelios a pain-killing injection so he could play on his injured groin muscle, but the shot numbed his hip and leg and made it impossible to skate.

Chelios had to watch a long, tense game, one of the most remarkable of the Avalanche's playoff run. When it ended, the Avalanche was back in business, Sakic re-directing Alexei Gusarov's sweet pass past a helpless Belfour at 4:33 of the third overtime.

How big was it? Huge. Immense. Gargantuan.

"If we had lost this game, the series might have been done," Ricci said.

The post-game verbal fireworks were almost as good as the game.

Roenick, miffed at a non-call when Sandis Ozolinsh tripped him during a breakaway in overtime, reacted acidly to a comment by Colorado goaltender Patrick Roy.

Roy suggested he would have stopped Roenick anyway. But Roenick recalled how he "left Roy's jock in the United Center rafters" during a breakaway goal in Game 3.

One day later, Roy said he couldn't hear Roenick's barbs because he had "two Stanley Cup rings plugging up" his ears.

The momentum now belonged to Colorado. Game 5 in Denver was as easy as Game 4 was difficult. Kamensky scored two goals, Roy was strong, and the Avalanche cruised to a 4-1 victory and a 3-2 lead.

The Blackhawks conceded nothing. "We're planning to win the next game and come back here for Game 7," Joe Murphy said. "We feel we're just as good a team as they are or better."

The Avalanche appeared to have Game 6 and the series sewn up after taking a 3-2 lead on Kamensky's goal 7:02 into the third period.

But this, clearly, was a series too good, too even to be determined in a mere 60 minutes. Murphy found the puck in the middle of a goalmouth scrum and slammed it past Roy with just 59.2 seconds left to tie the score.

The Avalanche, however, was undaunted. At 5:18 of the second overtime, Ozolinsh, the man brought in to provide offense from the blueline, sneaked in close, followed the rebound of his own shot and beat Belfour for the game-and series-winner.

A great game, a great series had ended on a great goal.

"Before I got here, I thought this team had the talent to win it all, but they had to improve on some things, especially the defensive play," Claude Lemieux said. "And we have. A series like this builds a team's character. You've got to find that extra drive you need to go all the way. We're maturing fast."

Yes . . . very fast.

Ripping the Red Wings

Defenseman Curtis Leschyshyn and the rest of his Avalanche teammates hardly stood in awe of the Detroit Red Wings, who recorded the best regular-season record in league history. Here, Leschyshyn smashes Darren McCarty in front of the net during the Avs' 4-2 victory at McNichols in Game 4.
Photo by Steve Dykes

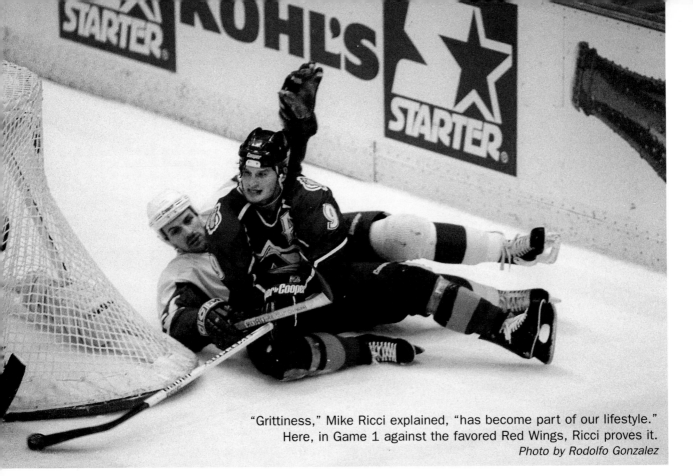

"Grittiness," Mike Ricci explained, "has become part of our lifestyle."
Here, in Game 1 against the favored Red Wings, Ricci proves it.
Photo by Rodolfo Gonzalez

Playoffs, Round Three: Detroit

The Detroit Red Wings.

This had to be the end of a long and often marvelous journey for the Avalanche, didn't it?

We were talking about the Detroit Red Wings, a team that had just come off the greatest regular season (62 wins) in the history of the game, a team fiercely motivated since it was swept a year earlier by the New Jersey Devils in the Cup Finals.

How long had Detroit waited for the Cup? Since 1955, longer than any other franchise. This was its year. The Avalanche, who finished 27 points behind the Red Wings during the regular season, would face a buzzsaw.

Except . . .

Except the Red Wings were suddenly looking very vulnerable. The Winnipeg Jets extended them to six games in the first round. The St. Louis Blues took them to the wall in Round Two, forcing them to seven games, and it took Detroit double overtime in Game 7 to win 1-0.

By the time the Avalanche and Red Wings met for Game 1 in Detroit, the home team was playing on legs as rubbery as the octopi their fans traditionally toss onto the ice. More than that, they were playing an Avalanche team that had discovered many good things about itself through the tortuous Chicago series.

Once again, overtime was the best time for Colorado. Mike Keane, another of general manager Pierre Lacroix's "character" acquisitions, put a screened wrist shot past Detroit goalie Chris Osgood at 17:31 of OT to give the Avalanche a 3-2 victory. Later, Mike Ricci observed, "Grittiness has become part of our lifestyle."

Surely, the proud, veteran Red Wings would bounce right back and put the big hurt on the upstart Avalanche in Game 2.

Wrong.

Colorado raised the level of its game even higher, throwing a 3-0 shutout at the Red Wings. Detroit was forced to play without its captain,

Steve Yzerman, and lost defenseman Paul Coffey to back spasms in the third period. But the way the Avalanche played, the way Patrick Roy blanketed the net, it was difficult to imagine the Wings winning even at full strength.

Warren Rychel, Sandis Ozolinsh and Joe Sakic scored three quick goals in the second period, and Roy made it stand up.

"I said before this series started that we were good enough to compete with this club," Claude Lemieux said. "The guys are getting hungrier and hungrier every game. It's a good sign when you see that the players want it as much as they do."

By now, Denver was a city possessed by the Avalanche, and the

team was showing more signs of championship mettle. The Avalanche wasn't only winning, it was winning the way teams have to in the playoffs: with defense and goaltending. Better yet, it was showing the kind of physical toughness some felt it lacked during the regular season.

Game 3, however, would prove an aberration. The Red Wings won a wild, sloppy 6-4 game at McNichols Arena, and Roy had his worst performance in recent memory. The Red Wings led 5-2 late in the first period and looked ready to put it on cruise control — until Adam Foote and Adam Deadmarsh scored quick goals at the end of the second period.

But just 32 seconds into the third period, Detroit defenseman Nicklas Lidstrom somehow beat Roy with a routine 62-foot shot, and the Wings held on for the victory.

The biggest noise, however, came after the game. That's when irascible Detroit coach Scotty Bowman waited in the parking lot and verbally ambushed Lemieux for what he felt was a sucker punch on Detroit's Slava Kozlov in Game 3.

Bowman enraged the Avalanche — not only with his ambush but with his incessant complaints about the glass, the boards and benches at McNichols. The next day, Avalanche coach Marc Crawford responded in a manner totally out of character: He ripped Bowman and joked that the plate in Bowman's head — the result of a horrid hockey injury — was causing interference in Avalanche coaches' headsets.

The NHL responded to Lemieux's sucker-punch by suspending the winger for Game 4.

The Avs had seen and heard enough. They

ABOVE: Winger Mike Keane scoots the puck down the ice. Keane's wrist shot slipped past Detroit goalie Chris Osgood in overtime, giving Colorado a shocking Game 1 victory in Detroit.
Photo by Rodolfo Gonzalez

proved it by overcoming Lemieux' suspension and winning 4-2 in Game 4 in Denver to go up 3-1. Deadmarsh, Lemieux' replacement, had a goal and an assist, and Roy rebounded from his lousy Game 3 performance.

Two nights later, the Red Wings made their last stand in front of their home folks, beating the Avalanche 5-2. Lemieux suggested that his team's performance be "thrown in the garbage can." The less said about the game the better, and the Avalanche knew it.

Game 6 in Denver would be the equivalent of Game 7. Nobody wanted to go back to Detroit. The Red Wings seemed to have found their legs after a slow start in this series, and the Avalanche needed to end it, now.

Before the game, the Avalanche, personified by the ever-cocky Roy, was supremely confident. "Well," he said, "Detroit won 62 games, they are entitled to win one game on their home ice." In other words: Roy, me worry?

No worry, no problem. The Avalanche was brilliant. Sakic was the best he's ever been, scoring two goals on remarkable solo efforts in a commanding 4-1 victory.

Big game, big performance, from the top of the Avalanche's roster to the bottom. The only dark moment came when Lemieux hit Detroit's Kris Draper from behind and sent him hurtling headfirst into the boards; Draper needed three hours of surgery to repair his face.

But nothing could dampen the Avalanche's spirits.

The underdog had bitten the big dog.

Denver was Cup Crazy, and the Avalanche was headed to the promised land — the Stanley Cup Finals.

LEFT: Jubilant Avs players bolt onto the ice as Game 6 ends and Colorado defeats Detroit, 4 games to 2, to win the Western Conference finals and reach the Stanley Cup Finals.
Photo by Rodolfo Gonzalez

BELOW: Joe Sakic lifts the Clarence Campbell Trophy after the Avs win the Western Conference finals against Detroit.
Photo by Hal Stoelzle

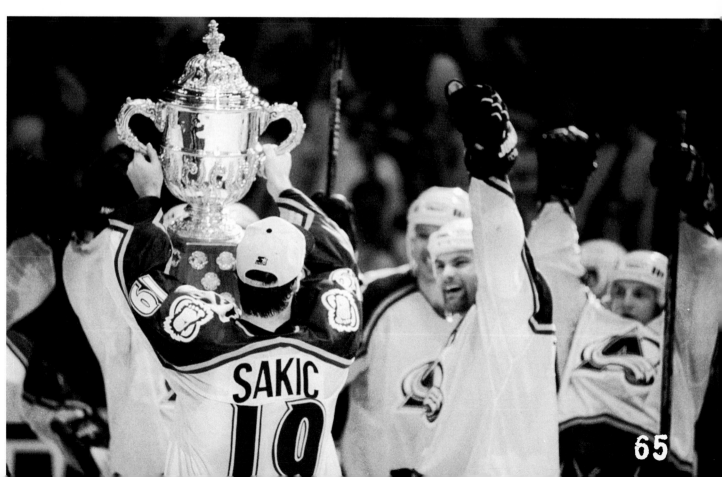

Champs at last, the Avs crowd around Claude Lemieux as he takes his turn holding the Stanley Cup after beating Florida 1-0 in triple overtime.
Photo by Hal Stoelzle

Seizing the Cup

The Avs and Panthers pile it on in Game 1 of the Stanley Cup Finals at McNichols Arena. *Photo by Rodolfo Gonzalez*

Stanley Cup Finals

Y ou think Stanley Cup Finals, you think traditional hockey markets: New York and Chicago. Detroit and Toronto. Montreal and Boston.

Colorado and Florida?

While the old-time hockey purists were rolling their eyes — or rolling in their graves — the National Hockey League was left with a Stanley Cup Final that represented the league's new surge into new markets.

Colorado and Florida: The Ski and Sea Series. Or something.

The Avalanche was a first-year team in Denver, transplanted after so many up-and-down years as the Quebec Nordiques. And Florida was a third-year team, an expansion club built by Islanders dynasty architect Bill Torrey.

The Panthers had somehow knocked off Philadelphia and Pittsburgh in back-to-back series. They had neutralized some of the game's greatest scorers, including Eric Lindros of the Flyers and Mario Lemieux and Jaromir Jagr of the Penguins.

The Panthers were the ultimate underdog —

GAME 1

Florida	1	0	0 — 1
Colorado	0	3	0 — 3

First Period — 1, Florida, Fitzgerald 4 (Lindsay), 16:51. Penalties — Mellanby, Fla (roughing), 9:12; Skrudland, Fla (roughing), 9:21; Krupp, col (high-sticking), 13:46; Gusarov, Col (holding), 18:15.

Second Period — 2, Colorado, Young 3 (Deadmarsh, Lefebvre), 10:32. 3, Colorado, Ricci 6 (Keene, Ozolinsh), 12:21. 4, Colorado, Krupp 3 (Kamensky, Forsberg), 14:20. Penalties — Svehla, Fla (interference), :41; Lindsay, Fla (roughing), 7:56; Ricci, Col (roughing), 15:31; Svehla, Fla (roughing), 17:39; Ricci, Col (goalie interference), 18:30.

Third Period — None. Penalties — Sakic, Col (holding), 3:35; Carkner, Fla (slashing), 6:51; Vanbiesbrouck, Fla, served by Sheppard (slashing), 9:55; Jovanovski, Fla (roughing), 19:42.

Shots on goal — Florida 12-6-8 — 26. Colorado 6-15-9 — 30. Power-play Opportunities — Florida 0 of 5; Colorado 0 of 8. Goalies — Florida, Vanbiesbrouck 12-7 (30 shots-27 saves). Colorado, Roy 13-6 (26-25). A — 16,061 (16,061). Referee — Bill McCreary. Linesmen — Ray Scapinello, Brian Murphy.

LEFT: The Panthers' Ed Jovanovski delivers his own brand of punishment to the Avs' Warren Rychel during Game 1.
Photo by Rodolfo Gonzalez

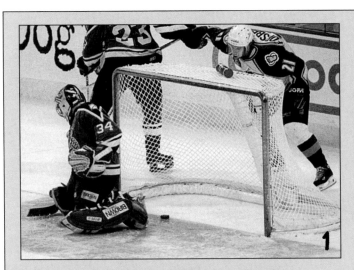

Peter Forsberg's three goals in the first period destroy Florida in Game 2, leading the Avs to an 8-1 victory and a commanding 2-0 lead. Panthers goalie John Vanbiesbrouck is Forsberg's victim (1). Forsberg completes his hat trick (2) with an assist from Adam Deadmarsh. Forsberg (center, 3) and Deadmarsh celebrate. Hats mark the hat trick (4) as a dejected Vanbiesbrouck waits for play to resume. Benched after giving up four goals, Vanbiesbrouck is overshadowed by Avs fans and their signs.

Forsberg's Hat Trick

or was it under-rat? — story in sports, a gritty group of overachievers who had reached the pinnacle with a close-checking, defensive style and a stellar goaltender named John Vanbiesbrouck.

The Panthers were making hockey the sport in South Florida, setting off a rat-loving frenzy in a town whose citizens didn't always know the color of the blueline.

The rat craze began during the regular season when winger Scott Mellanby killed a rat scurrying about the locker room before a game. Later, Mellanby scored two goals, moving Vanbiesbrouck to call it a "rat trick." A tradition was born.

The Panthers figured to be a formidable foe for Colorado. If they could stop Lindros, Lemieux and Jagr, couldn't they frustrate Joe Sakic and Peter Forsberg? And while the Avalanche had held the upper hand in goaltending the first three rounds, didn't Vanbiesbrouck figure to be Patrick Roy's equal, at the very least?

Worse yet, the Avs learned they would have to play the first two games of the Finals without Claude Lemieux, who was suspended, again, by the NHL, this time for his hit on Detroit's Kris Draper.

The Avalanche was favored, heavily favored, to win the Stanley Cup. But the memory of how the heavily favored Detroit Red Wings had been swept a season earlier by the defense-minded New Jersey Devils was still fresh.

Game 1 in Denver seemed to serve notice this would be yet another long, difficult and often frustrating series. The Panthers jumped on the Avalanche 1-0 and dominated the first period.

"We didn't pursue the puck very well, and we didn't finish very many checks," Avalanche coach Marc Crawford said.

The Avalanche, however, regained control in the second period with a quick-strike attack, getting three goals from Scott Young, Mike Ricci and Uwe Krupp. Suddenly, Vanbiesbrouck looked beatable. More, the Avs did the thing they knew they had to do: match Florida's work ethic.

Naturally, there was an off-ice conflagration, as there always is when the stakes are this high: A league official told Vanbiesbrouck moments before the game the red tape on his stick knob had to be replaced by white tape. Some trivial rule said so.

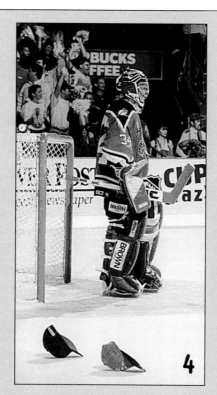

Photos by Cyrus McCrimmon (1, 2, 5),
Hal Stoelzle (3, 4)

Vanbiesbrouck changed the tape, and later, Florida coach Doug MacLean suggested the Avalanche had embarked on a dirty-tricks campaign. Crawford played the angel, saying, "I don't know anything about that."

By Game 2, it wouldn't have mattered whether Vanbiesbrouck had red tape, white tape — or a boat oar. The Avalanche was dominant.

Colorado had won Game 1 and had not played its best; this time, the Avs were awesome.

The Avalanche blew the Panthers out of McNichols 8-1, the second-most lopsided victory in Finals history. Peter Forsberg scored a first-period hat trick and Vanbiesbrouck, rattled, was removed after the first period.

"That was our 'A' game," Crawford said.

MacLean was stunned.

"I don't know how to explain it," he said after the Panthers' worst performance of the post-season — by far.

It all figured to change once the series moved to Miami Arena, now known as the Rat's Nest. South Florida had gone crazy over its hockey team, throwing plastic rats onto the ice after every

GAME 2

Florida	....	1 0 0 —	1
Colorado	....	4 3 1 —	8

First Period — 1, Colorado, Forsberg 8, 4:11. 2, Florida, Barnes 6 (Lowry, Jovanovski), 7:52 (pp). 3, Colorado, Corbet 2 (Young, Sakic), 10:43 (pp). 4, Colorado, Forsberg 9 (Sakic, Ozolinsh), 13:46 (pp). 5, Colorado, Forsberg 10 (Sakic, Deadmarsh), 15:05 (pp). Penalties — Deadmarsh, Col (roughing), 5:53; Lindsay, Fla (slashing), 8:55; Carkner, Fla (roughing), 12:51; Vanbiesbrouck, Fla, served by Mellanby (interference), 14:50.

Second Period — 6, Colorado, Corbet 3, 4:37. 7, Colorado, Kamensky 10 (Gusarov, Deadmarsh), 5:08. 8, Colorado, Klemm 1 (Corbet, Krupp), 10:03. Penalties — Lefebvre, Col (holding), 6:20; Rychel, Col (roughing), 17:01.

Third Period — 9, Colorado, Klemm 2 (Sakic), 17:28 (pp). Penalties — Kamensky, Col, double minor (high-sticking), 3:11; Jovanovski, Fla (roughing), 7:28; Kamensky, Col (roughing), 7:28; Leschyshyn, Col (charging), 7:28; Jovanovski, Fla, major (fighting), 9:39; Rychel, Col, minor-major-game misconduct (instigator, fighting), 9:39; Laus, Fla (interference), 11:42; Mellanby, Fla (roughing), 16:09.

Shots on goal — Florida 8-15-5 — 28. Colorado 11 — 12-7 — 30. Power-play Opportunities — Florida 1 of 7; Colorado 4 of 5. Goalies — Florida, Vanbiesbrouck 12-8 (11 shots-7 saves), Fitzpatrick (0:00 second, 19-15). Colorado, Roy 14-6 (28-27). A — 16,061 (16,061). Referee — Don Koharski. Linesmen — Kevin Collins, Gerard Gauthier.

Panthers goal.

As Game 3 neared, Miami was hot for hockey in anticipation of a host of "black rains" — the rats hitting the ice.

Only the rats didn't spend much time in the air.

Lemieux didn't waste any time in his return to the Finals, scoring the game's first goal. But the Panthers came back, taking a 2-1 lead in the first period, playing their best hockey of the series.

LEFT: Even Patrick Roy gives up a goal now and then. Panthers fans litter the Miami Arena ice with their trademark plastic rats after Florida scores during Game 3. But the Avs win 3-2 to take a 3-0 lead.
Photo by Rodolfo Gonzalez

Once again, the Avalanche owned the second period, getting goals from Mike Keane and Joe Sakic on consecutive shots in a span of 1:22, giving Colorado a 3-2 lead. Florida continued to press, but Roy was unbeatable, recalling memories of his post-season performances for Montreal in 1986 and 1993.

The best save came in the waning moments when Roy stuck out his left pad and stopped Mellanby from right in front of the net.

Mixing it up in front of the net, the Avs and Panthers play Game 4 like there's no tomorrow. And there isn't.
Photo by Rodolfo Gonzalez

The Avalanche held on to win 3-2 and took an insurmountable 3-0 lead in the series. History was on Colorado's side: Only one team in history, the 1942 Toronto Maple Leafs, had come back from three games down to win the Cup. It wasn't a question of whether the Avalanche was going to win the Cup, only when.

Come Game 4, the Avalanche decided, "The sooner the better."

From start to finish 104 minutes later, this was a goaltender's battle extraordinaire. Vanbiesbrouck played spectacularly, robbing Sandis Ozolinsh, Scott Young and every other Avalanche player one time or another.

Roy was equally impenetrable, stopping 63 shots. After 20 minutes, 40, 60, 80 and 100 minutes, the game was locked in a riveting scoreless tie.

And then it happened. At 4:31 of the third overtime, Krupp, who had come all the way back from a devastating knee injury suffered the first night of the season, sent a slap shot through a screen in front of Vanbiesbrouck. For a moment, he didn't know what had happened. And then he heard the shattering silence through the Miami Arena, and he knew. The puck was in. Game over.

Stanley Cup.

"I can only think, 'What a fortunate man I am,' " general manager

RIGHT: General manager Pierre Lacroix, architect of the champions, holds the Cup he helped win with his team-building strategy.
Photo by Hal Stoelzle

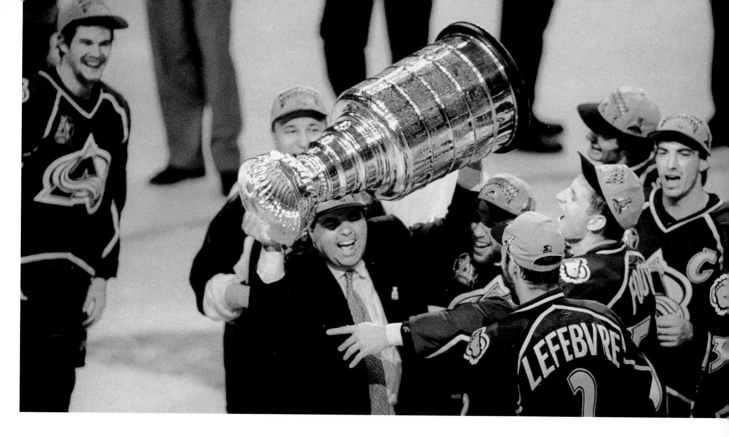

GAME 3

Colorado	1	2	0	—	3
Florida	2	0	0	—	2

First Period -1, Colorado, Lemieux 5 (Kamensky, Forsberg), 2:44. 2, Florida, Sheppard 8 (Straka, Jovanovski), 9:14 (pp). 3, Florida, Niedermeyer 5 (Mellanby, Garpenlov), 11:19. Penalties -Deadmarsh, Col (hooking), 7:40; Foote, Col (roughing), 12:49; Lowry, Fla (roughing), 12:49.

Second Period -4, Colorado, Keane 3 (Foote, Gusarov), 1:38. 5, Colorado, Sakic 18 (Deadmarsh, Leschyshyn), 3:00. Penalties -None.

Third Period -None. Penalties -None.

Shots on goal -Colorado 6-10-6 -22. Florida 16-13-5 -34. Power-play Opportunities -Colorado 0 of 0; Florida 0 of 1. Goalies -Colorado, Roy 15-6 (34 shots-32 saves). Florida, Vanbiesbrouck 12-9 (22-19). A -14,703 (14,703). Referee -Andy Van Hellemond. Linesmen -Ray Scapinello, Brian Murphy.

LEFT: Ripping the goal from its moorings, the Avs' Warren Rychel levels Florida's John Vanbiesbrouck in Game 4.
Photo by Rodolfo Gonzalez

ABOVE: The Stanley Cup and champagne: Life doesn't get any better than this for hockey players.
Photo by Rodolfo Gonzalez

Pierre Lacroix said, hugging the Cup. "How many people get to accomplish their dream?"

Joe Sakic said: "This is the greatest moment of my life."

Those sentiments would be echoed endlessly in a jubilant, champagne-soaked, cigar-smoke-filled locker room.

The team that was supposed to be a couple of years away was here, now, reveling in the moment.

Back in Denver, a town was going loony, engaging in an all-night street party it never wanted to end.

The long, strange, wonderful trip was complete.

Denver's first major pro sports championship had been secured.

The Cup was coming home.

GAME 4

Colorado	0	0	0	0	0	1	— 1
Florida	0	0	0	0	0	0	— 0

First Period — None. Penalty — Svehla, Fla. (roughing), 18:57.

Second Period — None. Penalties — Kamensky, Col (hooking), 5:21; Ozolinsh, Col (roughing), 5:21; Niedermayer, Fla. (roughing), 5:21; Foote, Col (roughing), 9:28; Jovanovski, Fla (cross-checking), 12:27; Leschyshyn, Col (hooking), 15:33; Ricci, Col (roughing), 18:05; Barnes, Fla (roughing), 18:05.

Third Period — None. Penalties — Vanbiesbrouck, Fla, served by Sheppard (interference), 5:15; Lemieux, Col (high-sticking), 6:29.

First Overtime — None. Penalties — Ozolinsh, Col (roughing), 13:04; Garpenlov, Fla (roughing), 13:04.

Second Overtime — None. Penalties — Lemieux, Col (slashing), 9:57; Skrudland, Fla (slashing), 9:57.

Third Overtime — 1, Colorado, Krupp, 4, 4:31. Penalties — None.

Shots on goal — Colorado 9-10-10-11-12—4—56. Florida 10-17-8-7-18-3—63. Power-play Opportunities — Colorado 0 of 3; Florida 0 of 4. Goalies — Colorado, Roy 16-6 (63 shots-63 saves). Florida, Vanbiesbrouck 12-10 (56-55). A — 14,703 (14,703). Referree — Bill McCreary. Linesmen — Kevin Collins, Gerard Gauther.

Tale of a team
PROFILES & STATS

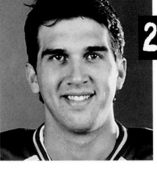

20 Rene Corbet

Position: left wing. **Age:** 22. **Height:** 6-0. **Weight:** 187.
Regular season: Recalled from Cornwall on Dec. 6 . . . Had three goals, six assists for Avs . . . Recorded two assists against Winnipeg on March 24.
Playoffs: Scored goal in first playoff appearance in eventual 5-4 victory in Game 5 of opening series against Vancouver. Finished with three goals, two assists in eight games.

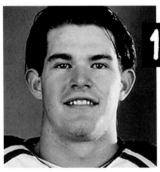

18 Adam Deadmarsh

Position: right wing. **Age:** 21. **Height:** 6-0. **Weight:** 195.
Regular season: Named First Star of the game against Philadelphia on Jan. 4, when he had one goal and one assist . . . Scored 30th career goal on April 3 against St. Louis . . . Got 50th career point with an assist against the New York Rangers on Feb. 3 . . . Third on team in penalty minutes (142).
Playoffs: Had 12 assists (tied for third on team) and five goals for 17 points (tied for fifth on team). Biggest contribution was in Game 4 of the Western Conference finals, when he replaced Claude Lemieux on the first line and had a goal and an assist.

35 Stephane Fiset

Position: goaltender. **Age:** 25. **Height:** 6-1. **Weight:** 195.
Regular season: Finished season with 22-6-7 record and 2.93 goals-against average, representing a personal best for victories . . . Stopped 44 of 46 shots against St. Louis on April 11 . . . Stopped all 37 shots by Boston on Jan. 9 to record first Avalanche shutout . . . Stopped 30 of 32 shots against Detroit on opening night, a 3-2 Colorado victory.
Playoffs: Did not play.

52 Adam Foote

Position: defenseman. **Age:** 24. **Height:** 6-1. **Weight:** 202.
Regular season: Recorded three-point game (one goal, two assists) on Feb. 29 against Chicago . . . Second Star of Jan. 4 game against Philadelphia . . . Scored goal in his first game of season on Oct. 9 against Pittsburgh . . . His plus/minus (+27) was third best on the team.
Playoffs: Played in all 22 games, scoring one goal and adding an assist . . . His 36 penalty minutes were second most on the team.

21 Peter Forsberg

Position: center. **Age:** 22. **Height:** 6-0. **Weight:** 190.
Regular season: Recorded points in 23 of the last 32 games of the season (14 goals-34 assists-48 points) . . . Ranked fifth in NHL in regular-season points with 116 . . . Ninth in NHL in shorthanded points with seven (3-4-7) . . . Fourth in NHL with 86 assists . . . Recorded multiple points in 33 games . . . Scored three or more points in 17 games . . . Scored points in eight consecutive games from Feb. 16-March 3 . . . Named to NHL All-Star team . . . Named NHL Player of the Month for February with nine goals and 16 assists. **Playoffs:** Played in all 22 games and tied for second on the team both in goals (10) and power-play goals (three) . . . Was third on team with 21 total points . . . Highlight was three-goal performance in Game 2 of the Finals.

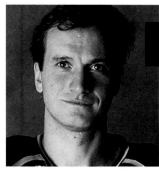

5 Alexei Gusarov

Position: defenseman. **Age:** 31. **Height:** 6-3. **Weight:** 185.
Regular season: Second on team in plus/minus with a +29 . . . Recorded career-high three assists against Anaheim on Feb. 26 . . . Played in his 200th NHL game on Jan. 6 . . . Missed two games with a concussion suffered Dec. 13 at Buffalo . . . Recalled from Cornwall on Oct. 6.
Playoffs: Played in 21 games and assisted on nine goals.

14 Dave Hannan

Position: center. **Age:** 34. **Height:** 5-10. **Weight:** 180.
Regular season: Acquired from Buffalo Sabres on March 20 in exchange for sixth-round draft choice in '96 . . . Recorded three multiple-point games during season . . . Scored his first goal with Avalanche on April 11 against St. Louis.
Playoffs: Played in 13 games, assisting on two goals.

13 Valeri Kamensky

Position: left wing. **Age:** 30. **Height:** 6-2. **Weight:** 198.
Regular season: Third on team with 85 points . . . Seventh in NHL and first on team with 18 power-play goals . . . Had hat tricks Dec. 5 against San Jose and March 20 against Los Angeles . . . Scored his 200th career point Jan. 14 at Calgary . . . Recorded 18 points in season's final 20 games . . . Scored in seven consecutive games from Dec. 1-13 . . . Scored first goal in Avalanche history on Oct. 6.
Playoffs: Played in all 22 games and was second on team with 22 points . . . Tied for second on team with 10 goals and three power-play goals . . . Scored two goals in fifth-game victory over Chicago.

25 Mike Keane

Position: right wing. **Age:** 29. **Height:** 5-10. **Weight:** 185.
Regular season: Acquired from Montreal in the Patrick Roy trade on Dec. 6 . . . Scored his 100th career goal on April 10 against Anaheim . . . Scored two goals on Dec. 15 against Hartford.
Playoffs: Played in all 22 games, scoring five points on three goals and two assists . . . Scored winning goal in overtime in opener of conference finals against Detroit . . . Scored in third game of Finals against Florida.

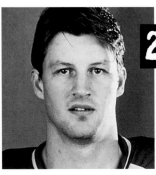

24 Jon Klemm

Position: defenseman. **Age:** 26. **Height:** 6-3. **Weight:** 200.
Regular season: Finished fifth among NHL rookies in plus/minus with a +12 . . . Recorded two assists against Ottawa on Dec. 9.
Playoffs: Played in 15 games, scoring two goals and adding an assist . . . One of his goals came on the power play.

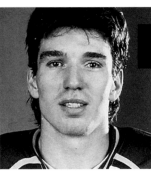

4 Uwe Krupp

Position: defenseman. **Age:** 30. **Height:** 6-6. Weight: 235.
Regular season: Injured his knee in season opener, underwent surgery on Oct. 21 and returned to action on April 6 against San Jose . . . Recorded two assists against Detroit before his injury . . . Avalanche was 5-1-0 with him in the lineup.
Playoffs: Played in all 22 games and tied for third on team with 12 assists . . . Scored two game-winning goals, including one that brought the Stanley Cup to Denver, in triple overtime of Game 4 at Florida.

2 Sylvain Lefebvre

Position: defenseman. **Age:** 28. **Height:** 6-2. **Weight:** 205.
Regular season: Recorded his 100th career point with assist against Pittsburgh on Jan. 16 . . . Missed six games with sprained right ankle suffered on Nov. 29 . . . Chosen First Star of the Feb. 26 game against Anaheim.
Playoffs: Played in all 22 games, assisting on five goals.

22 Claude Lemieux

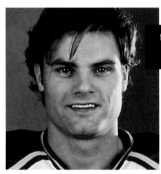

Position: right wing. **Age:** 30. **Height:** 6-1. **Weight:** 215.
Regular season: Recorded 18 points in last 20 games . . . Was third in NHL with 10 game-winning goals .
. . Ranked 20th in NHL with 39 goals scored . . . Scored in six consecutive games from Feb. 1-11 . . .
Recorded first hat trick ever by an Avalanche player on Nov. 28 against the Islanders . . . Scored in five
straight games from Oct. 27-Nov. 5 . . . Recorded his 250th NHL goal and 500th NHL point on Feb. 23.
Playoffs: Played in 19 games, scoring seven goals, three of them on the power play . . . Also added seven
assists, including three in the first game against Vancouver . . . Sat out three games (one against Detroit,
two against Florida) because of two suspensions.

7 Curtis Leschyshyn

Position: defenseman. **Age:** 26. **Height:** 6-1. **Weight:** 205.
Regular season: Ranked sixth in the NHL and first on the Avs with a plus/minus of +32, his second
straight season as the team's leader in that category . . . Logged his 100th NHL assist against Los Angeles
on March 20.
Playoffs: Played in 17 games, scoring one goal and assisting on two others.

10 Troy Murray

Position: center. **Age:** 33. **Height:** 6-1. **Weight:** 195.
Regular season: Played in 63 games despite injury-plagued season, scoring 21 points . . . Scored win-
ning goal against Montreal on Feb. 5 and two assists against Dallas on April 7.
Playoffs: Played in eight games but did not score.

8 Sandis Ozolinsh

Position: defenseman. **Age:** 23. **Height:** 6-3. **Weight:** 205.
Regular season: Recorded 18 points in final 16 games (4-14-18) . . . 15th among NHL defensemen and
tops among Avs defensemen with 54 points . . . Third on team in power-play points with eight goals and
24 assists . . . Acquired from San Jose in exchange for Owen Nolan on Oct. 26 . . . Tallied a season-high
four assists against his former teammates on March 28 . . . Got his 100th NHL assist on March 17
against Edmonton . . . Scored his 50th NHL goal against Montreal on Feb. 5.
Playoffs: Played in all 22 games and was second on the team with 14 assists . . . Added five goals, two of
them off the power play . . . Scored in second overtime of Game 6 to eliminate Blackhawks in second
round.

83

9 Mike Ricci

Position: center. **Age:** 24. **Height:** 6-0. **Weight:** 190.
Regular season: Recorded seven points, including six assists, in the season's final seven games . . . Played his 400th NHL game on March 5 against San Jose.
Playoffs: Played in all 22 games, scoring six goals with 11 assists . . . Scored two power-play goals in Game 5 loss to Detroit . . . Scores goal in Finals opener against Florida.

33 Patrick Roy

Position: goaltender. **Age:** 30. **Height:** 6-0. **Weight:** 192.
Regular season: Third in NHL with 34 victories (22 with Colorado), third-highest total in his career . . . On Feb. 19, became only the 12th goaltender, and the second-youngest, in league history to reach 300 victories . . . Acquired from Montreal on Dec. 6 . . . Recorded his 30th career shutout against Toronto (4-0) on March 3, stopping 26 shots . . . Stopped 43 of 45 shots against Ottawa on Feb. 25 . . . Stopped 37 of 39 shots against his former teammates on Feb. 5. **Playoffs:** Played all but one minute of playoffs, with a 2.10 goals-against average and a .921 save percentage . . . logged 649 saves throughout the playoffs . . . was 16-6, giving him a career playoff mark of 86-48 and three Stanley Cups.

16 Warren Rychel

Position: left wing. **Age:** 29. **Height:** 6-0. **Weight:** 202.
Regular season: Acquired from Toronto Maple Leafs on Oct. 2 . . . Finished second on team in penalty minutes with 147 . . . Played in his 200th NHL game on Dec. 5 against San Jose.
Playoffs: Played in 12 games, scoring one goal.

19 Joe Sakic

Position: center. **Age:** 26. **Height:** 5-11. **Weight:** 185.
Regular season: Set career highs of 51 goals, 69 assists and 120 points . . . Recorded nine goals and 13 assists in final 13 games . . . Sixth in NHL in goals and third in points . . . Fifth in NHL and first on Avs with 339 shots on goal . . . Second on team with 17 power-play goals . . . Scored multiple points in 36 games . . . Scored three-or-more points in 13 games . . . Scored seven straight games from Jan 27-Feb. 9 . . . Named to NHL All-Star team for the sixth consecutive season . . . Had two five-point games.
Playoffs: Played in all 22 games, recording 18 goals, 16 assists and 34 points, all team-highs . . . Six of his goals were game-winners . . . Scored hat trick, including game-winner in overtime, in Game 5 against Vancouver, then tied franchise record in next game with his seventh playoff goal, also the winner . . . Scored winner in third overtime of pivotal fourth game of the Chicago series . . . Scored two goals in clincher against Detroit.

12 Chris Simon

Position: left wing. **Age:** 24. **Height:** 6-3. **Weight:** 219.
Regular season: Scored points in final eight games of regular season . . . Led team in penalty minutes with 250 . . . Played in his 100th NHL game on Dec. 11 against Toronto . . . Tallied 31 penalty-minutes against Dallas on Nov. 9.
Playoffs: Played in only 12 games, scoring three points.

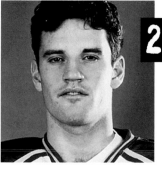

6 Craig Wolanin

Position: defenseman. **Age:** 28. **Height:** 6-3. **Weight:** 205.
Regular season: Scored career-high seven goals . . . Missed five games in December and January with injured right shoulder.
Playoffs: Played in seven games and scored one goal, a game-winner . . . Did not play after his giveaway led to winning Chicago goal in Game 3 of that second-round series.

26 Stephane Yelle

Position: center. **Age:** 22. **Height:** 6-1. **Weight:** 162.
Regular season: Led all NHL rookies in shorthanded points with four . . . Third among rookies with a plus/minus of +15 . . . Scored his first NHL goal on Nov. 1 against Calgary.
Playoffs: Played in all 22 games, scoring five points, including shorthanded goal.

48 Scott Young

Position: right wing. **Age:** 28. **Height:** 6-0. **Weight:** 190.
Regular season: Recorded seven points (2-5-7) in final six games . . . Recorded five three-point games. Tallied his 150th NHL goal on Feb. 5 against Montreal . . . Recorded his 200th NHL assist on Dec. 29 against Toronto.
Playoffs: Played in all 22 games and tied for third on team with 12 goals . . . Scored one of three Avalanche goals in Game 1 of the Finals against Florida.

Pierre Lacroix

Executive vice president of hockey operations/general manager

In only his second season as a general manager, Lacroix, 47, was named Executive of the Year by The Hockey News. In addition to hiring Marc Crawford as coach of his team before the 1994-95 season, Lacroix pulled off three major trades this season that helped the Avalanche win the Stanley Cup. He acquired Patrick Roy and Mike Keane from Montreal, Claude Lemieux from New Jersey and Sandis Ozolinsh from San Jose. Before joining the Quebec Nordiques/Colorado Avalanche, Lacroix was a player agent, representing such stars as Roy, Mike Bossy, Denis Savard, Robert Sauve and Alexandre Daigle.

Marc Crawford

Head coach

Selected coach of the year in his rookie season, Crawford, 35, actually surpassed his 1994-95 performance, when he led the Quebec Nordiques to the NHL's second-best record, with the franchise's first Stanley Cup season in 1995-96. In two seasons, his teams have compiled a 77-38-15 record. As a player, Crawford appeared in 176 regular-season and 20 playoff games during a seven-year career in the Vancouver Canucks organization.

CEO, Ascent Entertainment Group........................Charlie Lyons

Assistant General Manager ....François Giguere

Assistant Coach..Joel Quenneville

Assistant Coach..Jacques Cloutier

Athletic Trainer..Pat Karns

Equipment Manager..Rob McLean

1995-96 Regular Season Statistics

Head coach: Marc Crawford

POS	NO	PLAYER	GP	G	A	PTS	+/-	PIM	PP	SH	GW	OT	S	PCTG
C	19	Joe Sakic	82	51	69	120	14	44	17	6	7	1	339	15.0
C	21	Peter Forsberg	82	30	86	116	26	47	7	3	3	0	217	13.8
L	13	Valeri Kamensky	81	38	47	85	14	85	18	1	5	0	220	17.3
R	22	Claude Lemieux	79	39	32	71	14	117	9	2	10	0	315	12.4
R	48	Scott Young	81	21	39	60	2	50	7	0	5	0	229	9.2
D	8	Sandis Ozolinsh	73	14	40	54	2	54	8	1	1	1	166	8.4
C	18	Adam Deadmarsh	78	21	27	48	20	142	3	0	2	0	151	13.9
L	12	Chris Simon	64	16	18	34	10	250	4	0	1	0	105	15.2
C	26	Stephane Yelle	71	13	14	27	15	30	0	2	1	0	93	14.0
R	25	Mike Keane	73	10	17	27	5-	46	0	2	2	0	84	11.9
D	6	Craig Wolanin	75	7	20	27	25	50	0	3	0	0	73	9.6
C	9	Mike Ricci	62	6	21	27	1	52	3	0	1	0	73	8.2
C	10	Troy Murray	63	7	14	21	15	22	0	0	1	0	36	19.4
D	5	Alexei Gusarov	65	5	15	20	29	56	0	0	0	0	42	11.9
D	7	Curtis Leschyshyn	77	4	15	19	32	73	0	0	1	0	76	5.3
C	14	Dave Hannan	61	7	10	17	3	32	1	1	2	0	41	17.1
D	52	Adam Foote	73	5	11	16	27	88	1	0	1	0	49	10.2
D	2	Sylvain Lefebvre	75	5	11	16	26	49	2	0	0	0	115	4.3
D	24	Jon Klemm	56	3	12	15	12	20	0	1	1	0	61	4.9
L	20	Rene Corbet	33	3	12	15	12	20	0	1	1	0	61	4.9
L	16	Warren Rychel	52	6	2	8	6	147	0	0	1	0	45	13.3
D	4	Uwe Krupp	6	0	3	3	4	4	0	0	0	0	9	0.0

Goaltenders

NO	PLAYER	GP	MIN	AVG	W-L-T	EN	SO	GA	SA	SV%	G	A	PIM
33	Patrick Roy	39	2305	2.68	12-15-1	3	1	103	1130	.909	0	0	4
35	Stephane Fiset	37	2107	2.93	22-6-7	3	1	103	1012	.898	0	1	2
Totals		82	4982	2.89	47-25-10	6	2	240	2370	.899	0	1	6

1995-96 Playoff Statistics

POS	NO	PLAYER	GP	G	A	PTS	+/-	PIM	PP	SH	GW	OT	S	PCTG
C	19	Joe Sakic	22	18	16	34	10	14	6	0	6	2	98	18.4
C	21	Peter Forsberg	22	10	11	21	10	18	3	0	1	0	50	20.0
L	13	Valeri Kamensky	22	10	12	22	11	28	3	0	2	0	56	17.9
R	22	Claude Lemieux	19	5	7	12	5	55	3	0	0	0	81	6.2
R	48	Scott Young	22	3	12	15	6	10	0	0	0	0	61	4.9
D	8	Sandis Ozolinsh	22	5	14	19	5	16	2	0	1	1	52	9.6
C	18	Adam Deadmarsh	22	5	12	17	8	25	1	0	0	0	40	12.5
L	12	Chris Simon	12	1	2	3	2-	11	0	0	0	0	9	11.1
C	26	Stephane Yelle	22	1	4	5	2	8	0	1	0	0	24	4.2
R	25	Mike Keane	22	3	2	5	1	16	0	0	1	1	22	13.6
D	6	Craig Wolanin	7	1	0	1	2	8	0	0	1	0	5	20.0
C	9	Mike Ricci	22	6	11	17	1-	18	3	0	1	0	31	19.4
C	10	Troy Murray	8	0	0	0	4-	19	0	0	0	0	6	0.0
D	5	Alexei Gusarov	21	0	9	9	13	12	0	0	0	0	15	0.0
D	7	Curtis Leschyshyn	17	1	2	3	4	8	0	0	0	0	9	11.1
C	14	Dave Hannan	13	0	2	2	3	2	0	0	0	0	2	0.0
D	52	Adam Foote	22	1	3	4	11	36	0	0	0	0	20	5.0
D	2	Sylvain Lefebvre	22	0	5	5	4	12	0	0	0	0	22	0.0
D	24	Jon Klemm	15	2	1	3	6	0	1	0	1	0	11	18.2
L	20	Rene Corbet	8	3	2	5	3	2	1	0	1	0	4	25.0
L	16	Warren Rychel	12	1	0	1	4	23	0	0	0	0	4	25.0
D	4	Uwe Krupp	22	4	12	16	5	33	1	0	2	1	38	10.5

Goaltenders

NO	PLAYER	GP	MIN	AVG	W-L-T	EN	SO	GA	SA	SV%	G	A	PIM
33	Patrick Roy	22	1454	2.10	16-6	0	3	51	649	.921	0	0	0
35	Stephane Fiset	1	1	0.00	0-0	0	0	0	0	.000	0	0	0
Totals		22	1460	2.10	16-6	0	3	51	649	.921	0	0	0

Regular season
Game-by-Game Highlights

OCTOBER

Date	Opponent	Result	Highlight
6	Detroit	W, 3-2	Valeri Kamensky's second goal with 3:53 left wins opener.
7	@Los Angeles	L, 4-2	Vitali Yachmenev scores two goals to lead Kings.
9	Pittsburgh	T, 6-6	Teams total 72 shots; Jaromir Jagr ties it in final 81 seconds.
11	Boston	W, 3-1	Stephane Fiset stops 34 of 35 shots; Peter Forsberg, two assists.
13	@Washington	L, 3-1	Jim Carey stops 25 of 26 shots; Joe Sakic scores only Avs goal.
14	@St. Louis	L, 4-1	Blues score two short-handed goals; Avs 1-for-10 on power play.
18	Washington	W, 4-2	Avalanche beats Carey early with two goals in first, two in second.
23	Anaheim	W, 3-1	Mike Ricci, Adam Deadmarsh and Kamensky score in first period.
25	@Calgary	W, 3-2	Colorado wins on the road for first time, extends win streak to three.
27	Buffalo	W, 5-4	Forsberg has two goals, assist; Claude Lemieux gets winning goal.
30	@Dallas	W, 6-1	Sakic has two goals, two assists as Avs win fifth straight.

NOVEMBER

Date	Opponent	Result	Highlight
1	Calgary	W, 6-1	Lemieux scores twice to keep Avalanche unbeaten at home.
3	@Winnipeg	W, 5-2	Avalanche outshoots Winnipeg 48-26; Lemieux scores twice.
5	@Chicago	W, 7-3	Colorado sets club record with eighth straight victory.
9	Dallas	T, 1-1	Unbeaten streak extended to nine games; Troy Murray gets goal.
11	@Vancouver	W, 8-4	Forsberg scores twice; Avalanche wins fifth straight road game.
15	@Anaheim	L, 7-3	Unbeaten streak ends at 10; Jocelyn Thibault takes loss.
17	@Calgary	W, 5-3	Fiset makes 44 saves; Sakic and Forsberg among five Avs who score.
18	Calgary	W, 5-2	Fiset wins ninth straight; Colorado improves to 7-0-2 at home.
20	@Edmonton	T, 3-3	Colorado loses 3-1 lead as Edmonton's Doug Weight scores hat trick.
22	Chicago	W, 6-2	Five different Avs score; Fiset gets 12th victory.
25	@Montreal	T, 2-2	Sandis Ozolinsh salvages a tie with third-period goal.
28	@N.Y. Islanders	W, 7-3	Lemieux collects Avalanche's first hat trick.
29	@New Jersey	L, 4-3	Stephane Richer scores in overtime to beat Avs.

DECEMBER

Date	Opponent	Result	Highlight
1	@NY Rangers	L, 5-3	Mike Richter makes 38 saves; Avs lose second in a row.
3	Dallas	L, 7-6	Stars snap 25-game home unbeaten streak dating back to Quebec.
5	San Jose	W, 12-2	Kamensky's hat trick helps Avs end three-game losing streak.
7	Edmonton	L, 5-3	Edmonton spoils Patrick Roy's debut in Denver.
9	@Ottawa	W, 7-3	Fiset makes 20 saves; Forsberg has two goals, three assists.
11	@Toronto	W, 5-1	Roy makes 30 saves for his first Avs win, 290th overall.
13	@Buffalo	L, 4-3	Avs fall behind 3-0 in first, lose penalty-filled game.
15	@Hartford	L, 4-2	Mike Keane scores two goals; Avs 0-for-5 on power play.
18	Vancouver	L, 4-2	Roy's 27 saves only bright spot in Avs' third straight loss.
20	@Edmonton	W, 4-1	Sakic scores twice; Roy makes 28 saves.
22	St. Louis	W, 2-1	Lemieux shuts down Brett Hull; Roy wins first at home.
23	@Los Angeles	T, 2-2	Sakic scores two goals; Fiset makes 36 saves.
26	@San Jose	W, 5-1	Kamensky gets 17th and 18th goals; Roy, 28 saves.
29	Toronto	W, 3-2	Sakic and Scott Young get goal, two assists each.

JANUARY

Date	Opponent	Result	Highlight
3	New Jersey	L, 1-0	Martin Brodeur makes 30 saves in shutting out Avalanche.
4	Philadelphia	T, 2-2	Kjell Samuelsson scores with 4:03 left to tie Avs.
6	@Toronto	L, 5-2	Sakic scores 28th goal in loss; Avs outshot 35-28.
9	@Boston	W, 3-0	Sakic, Forsberg, Deadmarsh score; Fiset makes 37 saves.
10	Florida	T, 4-4	Avs score three in third to salvage tie; Young, two goals.
13	Calgary	T, 4-4	German Titov scored with 45 seconds left to give Calgary a tie.
16	@Pittsburgh	W, 5-2	Lemieux's hat trick gives Avalanche win.
17	@Detroit	L, 3-2	Steve Yzerman scores 500th goal in Detroit victory.
22	NY Islanders	W, 4-3	Roy makes 31 saves; Avs break home winless streak.
25	Vancouver	T, 2-2	Avs give up two third-period goals for fifth tie in 13 games.
27	@San Jose	W, 4-3	Kamensky scores game-winner in overtime.
31	@Anaheim	L, 2-1	Anaheim snaps Avs' three-game unbeaten streak.

FEBRUARY

Date	Opponent	Result	Highlight
1	Winnieg	W, 6-4	Lemieux scores two goals and adds an assist.
3	N.Y. Rangers	W, 7-1	Sakic scores goals 34 and 35; home unbeaten streak at seven.
5	Montreal	W, 4-2	Roy makes 37 saves in first game against his former team.
7	Tampa Bay	T, 4-4	Sakic has goal (36) and two assists in tie.
9	Hartford	L, 3-2	Roy denied 300th career victory in overtime loss.
11	@Philadelphia	W, 5-3	Forsberg gets first career hat trick.
15	@Tampa Bay	L, 4-2	Roy misses 300th again; Sakic and Keane score for Avs.
16	@Florida	W, 5-4	Avs score four straight, win in OT; Keane gets game-winner.
19	Edmonton	W, 7-5	Roy gets career win No. 300. Joins 11 previous net-minders.
23	Los Angeles	W, 6-2	Forsberg gets five assists; Lemieux, Kamensky score 28th each.
25	Ottawa	W, 4-2	Forsberg scores 25th; Roy makes 43 saves.
26	Anaheim	W, 3-2	Roy gets 302nd win, tied for 11th all-time.
29	@Chicago	L, 4-3	Avs' five-game winning streak snapped.

MARCH

Date	Opponent	Result	Highlight
1	Chicago	W, 5-3	Four unanswered goals lift Avs; Lemieux scores two goals.
3	Toronto	W, 4-0	Roy gets first shutout as an Av, stopping 26 shots.
5	San Jose	L, 5-3	Wade Flaherty stopped 57 shots for San Jose.
8	Detroit	L, 4-2	Forsberg and Sakic scored a goal apiece in the loss.
9	@Vancouver	W, 7-5	Lemieux scored goals 32 and 33 in Avs win.
13	@Anaheim	L, 4-0	Guy Hebert made 27 saves, Baleri Karpov scored twice for Anaheim.
17	Edmonton	W, 8-1	Sakic scored his 43rd goal and had four assists in the win.
19	@Vancouver	W, 4-3	Chris Simon scored his career-high 13th goal.
20	@Los Angeles	W, 5-2	Kamensky scored second hat trick, Forsberg got 81st assist.
22	@Detroit	L,7-0	Avs clinch division title despite loss.
24	@Winnipeg	W, 5-2	Sakic's two first-period goals lead Avs.
27	Winnipeg	L, 3-1	Sakic scores 46th goal in loss.
28	@San Jose	W, 8-3	Sakic's two goals and one assist give him career-high 111 points.

APRIL

Date	Opponent	Result	Highlight
3	St. Louis	L, 6-3	Third loss in five games; Deadmarsh, Kamensky and Simon score.
6	San Jose	W, 5-1	Stephane Yelle scores two goals; Rychel adds one.
7	@Dallas	W, 4-1	Sakic gets goal No. 50, Avs win third-straight.
10	Anaheim	W, 7-3	Keane scores two for 99th and 100th of career.
11	@St. Louis	W, 3-2	Fiset saves 44, Avs tie franchise mark for wins and points.
14	Los Angeles	L, 5-4	Avs lose in OT, four-game winning streak snapped.

EXTRA

DENVER

Rocky Mountain News

An edition of the 🏛 Rocky Mountain News

ROY-HOOOO!

Hans Deryk/Associated Press

Patrick Roy, shown at the end of Game 3, lived up to his billing as the NHL's greatest playoff goaltender by leading the Colorado Avalanche to its first Stanley Cup.

Front page of the Rocky Mountain News extra edition after the Avalanche swept Florida to win the Stanley Cup.

Photo by Glenn Asakawa

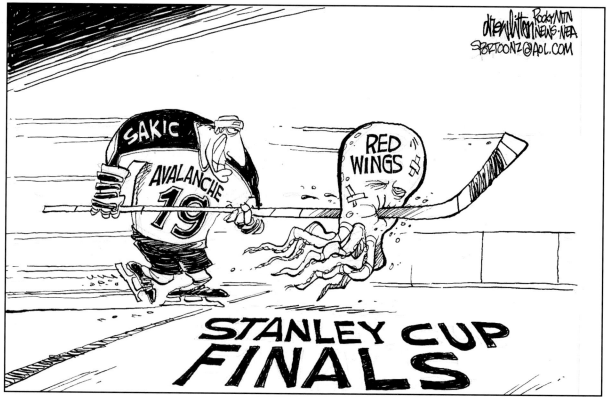

Photo by Rodolfo Gonzalez

ABOUT THE AUTHOR

Bob Kravitz, 36, is the *Rocky Mountain News*' lead sports columnist. He
has written for the paper since 1990. He is the author of *Mile High Madness*,
an account of the Colorado Rockies' inaugural season. He has worked at *The
(Cleveland) Plain Dealer, Sports Illustrated, Pittsburgh Press, San Diego Union*
and *The* (N.J.) *Record.* He lives in Littleton with his wife Cathy and daughters
Michelle and Dana.

Published in the United States by Johnson Books, a Division of Johnson Publishing Company, 1880 South 57th Court, Boulder, Colorado 80301.

9   8   7   6   5   4   3   2   1

Library of Congress Cataloging-in-Publication Data on file
LC 96-77391
ISBN 1-55566-185-8
Color Separations by Impressive Images, Fort Collins, Colorado
Printed in the United States by Johnson Printing, 1880 South 57th Court, Boulder, Colorado 80301.

 Printed on recycled paper with soy ink.